"Every year, for a number of years, I make a point of meeting with Dan Kennedy for a day, sometimes two days. His insights into progressively taking my businesses to the next level, and the next, and the next are invaluable."

—Michael Jans, Insurance Profit Systems, Oregon, www.quantumclub.com
(Mr. Jans is a leading consultant and coach to business owners in the property and casualty insurance industry.)

"Month after month, I keep saying 'thank you' to Dan Kennedy for everything his marketing ideas have done for my businesses."

—William Hammond, Attorney, Kansas, www.elderlaw.com
(Mr. Hammond is an elder law attorney in private practice, an author, and a business advisor to other attorneys.)

"In 2001, we had two stores . . . we were working like dogs and barely keeping $50,000.00 a year . . . . and, that year, we were threatened by a big box discount chain coming to town. In 2003, our two stores are thriving, we have a growing internet and mail-order business, our income has increased by more than 400%, and we are finally working sane hours. The difference? Dan Kennedy's marketing strategies."

—Charles and Betty Hildegarb, Antiquities LLC, Georgia

"Dan Kennedy completely and radically changed my entire business—I now make a much larger income with much less work. And I'm showing agents all over the country how to clone my business."

—Rob Minton, Realtor, Home Selling Team Inc., www.IncomeForLife.com

"My friend Dan Kennedy is unique, a genius in many ways. I have always admired his ability to see the vital truths in any business and to state these realities with straight language and clear definitions. His approach is direct. His ideas are controversial. His ability to get results for his clients is unchallenged. "

—Brian Tracy, from his introduction to Dan's *No B.S. Business Success* book (Brian Tracy is one of America's most sought after speakers and the author of dozens of business books. www.BrianTracy.com)

"Dan has literally eliminated the B.S. in explaining great ways to make more sales."

—Tom Hopkins, from his introduction to Dan's *No B.S. Sales Success* book (Tom Hopkins is world-renowned as a master sales trainer. www.TomHopkins.com)

"If you want to make money, get your Ph.E.—rush to your nearest bookstore and get Dan Kennedy's new book*— it's like a four year course in Entrepreneurship!"

(*Refers to Dan's book *How to Make Millions with Your Ideas*.)
—Al Ries, author, *Marketing Warfare* and *22 Immutable Laws of Marketing*

"Kennedy offers counter-intuitive advice . . . might give some people the necessary nudge to earn a few million dollars."

—*Publishers Weekly*, refers to Dan's book *No Rules: 21 Giant Lies About Success*

N●B.S.
DIRECT
MARKETING

N⊘B.S.
DIRECT
MARKETING

THE ULTIMATE
NO HOLDS BARRED
KICK BUTT
TAKE NO PRISONERS
DIRECT MARKETING
FOR NON-DIRECT
MARKETING BUSINESSES

Dan Kennedy

Ep
Entrepreneur®
Press

Editorial Director: Jere L. Calmes
Cover Design: David Shaw
Production and Composition: Eliot House Productions

This publication is designed to provide accurate and authoritative information in regard to the subject matter covered. It is sold with the understanding that the publisher is not engaged in rendering legal, accounting or other professional services. If legal advice or other expert assistance is required, the services of a competent professional person should be sought.

Library of Congress Cataloging-in-Publication Data
Kennedy, Dan S., 1954-
 No b.s. direct marketing: the ultimate, no holds barred, kick butt, take no prisoners direct marketing for non-direct marketing businesses/by Dan S. Kennedy.
  p.   cm.
 ISBN 13 : 978-193253157-2 (alk. paper)
 ISBN 10 : 1-932531-57-2 (alk. paper)
 1. Direct marketing. I. Title.
HF5415.126.K46 2006
658.8'72—dc22   2005032076

Printed in Canada
12 11 10 09 08   10 9 8 7 6 5

Contents

SECTION II

INSIDE NON-DIRECT MARKETING
BUSINESSES SUCCESSFULLY
USING DIRECT MARKETING

SECTION III

RESOURCES

Preface
The End of Advertising and Marketing as You Know It

Most small business advertising and marketing stinks. Monstrous sums are wasted, and opportunities lost.

Most businesspeople are floundering around, uncertain of even the difference between "good" advertising and marketing and "bad" advertising and marketing.

Pretty much everything you think you know about this is wrong. Everything you see big companies doing isn't right for you. Your peers and competitors are the blind leading the blind.

This book presents a radical prescription for change.

If you get it, you'll smack yourself in the head for not seeing it all sooner, on your own. You'll be in awe of how much sense it makes. You'll never look at an ad, sales letter, flier, etc. the same way again. You'll be ruined toward traditional advertising for life.

You will make major changes in your own advertising and market-ing—fast.

When you do, you will be criticized, argued with, and probably laughed at by competitors, employees, maybe even family and friends. You will get such astounding results, however, that you will have the courage and discipline to ignore them all. Being thought a fool or a misguided renegade and having millions of dollars is better than being thought "normal" and "correct" and barely making a living.

I get nearly obscene sums of money to advise entrepreneurs on direct marketing, to write sales copy for them, and to otherwise assist them with assembling marketing plans and tools. I tell you this not to brag, but to impress on you the extremely high value of the book you are starting to read. For example, I am routinely paid upwards of $50,000.00 to $100,000.00 plus royalties to craft sales letters and ad campaigns for clients, over 85% of whom use me repeatedly. Beginning in 2006, it became necessary to join a Private Client Group, for a fee, to be certain of being able to hire me. And my base fee for a day of consulting, pure question/answer conversation, is $9,200.00. The core elements of all my advice to all these clients is well represented in this book, even though I have written only a few of its chapters.

In this book, I've assembled a cast of other authors, each contributing one chapter. It is an eclectic group. All have at some point renounced traditional, normal advertising and marketing and converted to my approach. Some were converted easily, others with great angst, resistance, and skepticism. Some have become exceptionally adept at using this unusual marketing in their own businesses. Most have also gone on to prominence and leadership as advisors to others in their industries or professions. They are all radical revolutionaries. Were it a different time, their peers and competitors might declare them witches and burn them at the stake.

You can profit from all of them, from every chapter. But you should find one or two chapters very specifically matched to your particular type of business. The chapters specific to your type of business will likely be of the most obvious, direct, and immediate interest and value, with items you can apply and act on with little or no translation. However, the sum total of all the chapters will not only alter specific marketing modus operandi in your business, it will also alter your mindset about marketing. And the impact of all these authors on the way you think about marketing may very well be of even greater value than the impact of the advice targeted specifically to your type of business. In short, this book includes a small, thin handbook comprised of a chapter or two that is specific to your business and has definite things to do and a much larger, even global, discussion aimed at altering the way you think about marketing, from A to Z. Although this is a book about "marketing," you are about to make discoveries that will change your entire life.

But don't take my word for it. Read the comments at the start of the book, representative of thousands in my possession. Then get started. An eye-popping, jaw-dropping adventure awaits.

Book Road Map

Section I. Here is my crash course on direct marketing as it can be applied to any business, sales career, or professional practice.

Learning or reviewing these basic fundamentals lays the foundation for getting maximum value from the chapters written by different experts in Section II.

SECTION II. These chapters have been provided by different authors, each a successful business owner and advisor to business owners in different fields. You will almost certainly find that one of these chapters perfectly or closely matches your business, and you can jump to reading that first if you like. But you will find ideas that will translate to your business in all of these chapters.

SECTION III. Here are resources and references, beginning with FREE things you are entitled to as owner of this book, including two free tickets (valued at $995.00 each) to a giant Marketing and Wealth Seminar, an e-mail course, and other online tools, as well as a free, three-month Gold Membership to my Inner Circle. Contact information for just about everyone mentioned in this book appears in this section as well. IMPORTANT NOTE: The free e-mail course, at www.nobsbooks.com, is an extension of this book.

LAYING THE FOUNDATION
FOR EXCEPTIONAL SUCCESS
Applying Direct Marketing
to Any Business

CHAPTER 1

The Big Switch

Why Direct Marketing for NON-Direct Marketing Businesses?

I t is an odd sort of title, isn't it?

If you picked it up hoping for huge breakthroughs in your business, you bought the right book.

But first, I have to get these definitions out of the way.

By non-direct marketing business, I mean anything *but* a mail-order, catalog, or online marketer who *directly* solicits orders for merchandise.

Examples of direct marketing businesses just about everybody knows are the TV home shopping channels, QVC and HSN, Home Shopping Network; catalogers like Lillian Vernon, J. Peterman, and SkyMall; businesses like Fruit of the Month Club; and mass users of direct-mail to sell things like Publishers Clearinghouse. There are tens of thousands of true direct marketing businesses. Some are familiar to the general public; many, many more are familiar only to the niche or special interest they serve. For example, I have over 50 direct marketers as clients, each selling books, audio CDs, home study courses, and seminars and services by mail, internet, and print media, and teleseminars, which telemarket only to a specific industry or profession—one to carpet cleaners, another to restaurant owners, another to chiropractors, etc. If you are not a chiropractor, you don't know the name Dr. Ben Altadonna. If you are a chiropractor, it would be hard not to know of him, thanks to his full-page ads in the industry trade journals, massive amounts of direct mail, and other direct marketing. There are also direct marketers unknown by name but known by their products or brands, like a long-time client of mine, Guthy-Renker Corporation, the billion-dollar business behind TV infomercials for Victoria Principal's Principal Secret skin care products and Pro-Activ acne creams. Or my friend Joe Sugarman, the direct marketing genius who owns Blu-Blockers sunglasses, which are sold on QVC, via infomercials, the internet, and direct-mail, as well as in stores. What all these have in common is their fundamental process of selling direct via media to consumers, with no bricks 'n mortar locations or face-to-face contact required.

These are *not* the folks this book is for, even if they are the kinds of entrepreneurs I work personally with the most.

This book is for the owner of a bricks 'n' mortar business, a business with a store, showroom or office, a restaurant, a dental practice, an accounting practice, or a funeral home, that is some kind of ordinary business, one most likely local and serving a local market. These are the entrepreneurs who have populated my audiences for two decades, subscribe to my *No B.S. Marketing Letter,* and use my systems to transform those "ordinary" businesses into extraordinary money machines that far, far out-perform their industry norms, peers, competitors, and their own wildest imaginations. How do they do it? The big switch is a simple one to state (if more complex to do): they switch from traditional advertising to *direct-response* advertising. They stop emulating ordinary and traditional marketing and instead emulate *direct* marketing.

Don't wait. Right now, go to www.nobs books.com, click FREE NEWSLETTER, and enroll for three months' of my *No B.S. Marketing Letter* and my monthly Audio CD, FREE. Also, sign up for the FREE e-mail course that extends and expands on this book.

Most "ordinary" businesses advertise and market much like bigger brand-name companies, so they spend (waste) a lot of money on image, brand, and presence. But copycatting these big brand-name companies is like a rabbit behaving like the lion. It makes no sense. The big companies have all sorts of reasons for the way they advertise and market that have nothing to do with getting a customer or making sales! Because your agenda is much simpler, so you should find successful businesses with similar agendas to copycat. Those are direct marketers. You and they share the same basic ideas:

1. Spend a $1.00 on marketing, get back $2.00 or $20.00, fast, that can be accurately tracked to the $1.00 spent.
2. Do NOT spend $1.00 that does not directly and quickly bring back $2.00 or $20.00.

Big Company's Agenda for Advertising and Marketing

1. Please/appease its board of directors (most of whom know zip about advertising and marketing but have lots of opinions)

2. Please/appease its stockholders

3. Look good, look appropriate to Wall Street

4. Look good, appropriate to the media

5. Build brand identity

6. Win awards for advertising

7. Sell something

Your Agenda

1. Sell something. Now.

Please stop to be sure you get this life-changing principle. Be careful who you copy. Be careful who you act like. Be careful who you study. If their purpose, objectives, agenda, and reasons for doing what they do the way they do it doesn't match with your purpose, objectives, and agenda, then you should NOT study or emulate or copy them!

Please stop to be sure you get this life-changing corollary principle. Find somebody who is successful, who shares your purpose, objectives, agenda, and pay great attention to what he does and how he does it.

I believe some call this sort of thing "a blinding flash of the obvious." Well, you can call it obvious if you like—but then how do you explain the fact that 99% of all businesspeople are operating as if ignorant of this obvious logic?

And, I might add, this principle has power in places other than marketing. You *can* eventually get south by going due north, but life's easier and less stressful, and business more profitable, if you actually get headed in the direction that leads to your destination of choice. Emulating inappropriate examples is the equivalent of trudging south to get to the North Pole. Odds are, you'll get lost, tired, or eaten by a giant iguana long before seeing snow.

Why Is There so Much Lousy, Unproductive, Unprofitable Advertising and Marketing Out There, Anyway?

No B.S. truth. Most business owners are just about clueless when it comes to advertising and marketing. They are, therefore, often Advertising Victims, preyed on by media salespeople and ad agencies and others who don't know any more about how to actually produce a customer or make a sale than they do! If you

try to get a business owner to accurately tell you where his customers and sales come from, what it costs to get a customer from
source A or source B, or what results specifically come from this
ad or that one, he can't. He's guessing. Consequently, he's often
grumpy and unhappy about things he shouldn't be and also
wasting money he needn't be.

The reasons for the cluelessness and vulnerability to victim-
ization are many. Here's a big one: Marketing Incest. When you
got into whatever business you're in, you probably looked
around at what everybody else in the business was doing and
copied it. Gradually, you've tried to do it better, but not radically
different, just better. So you have everybody in an industry
standing in a circle looking inward at each other, ignoring anyone or anything outside the circle. It's incestuous, and it works
just like real generational incest: Everybody slowly gets dumber
and dumber and dumber.

All of the people you'll meet in this book did something very
different. They turned their backs on the circle and deliberately
went far afield from their peers in search of different—not just
incrementally better—but different ways of marketing. Now you
will, too.

Yes, Salvation Is Within Reach

Now, here's the good news: most business owners, clueless as
they may be about profitable advertising or effective marketing,
do know a lot about how to *sell* their products or services. That's
very good news because DIRECT *Marketing for NON-Direct
Marketing Businesses* is really not about traditional advertising or
marketing at all. It is simply "salesmanship multiplied in

media." So you actually already do have a firm grip on one-third of the KENNEDY RESULTS TRIANGLE that you'll master with this book. You know the Message. It'll get tweaked, as I'll explain. But you do have this component part.

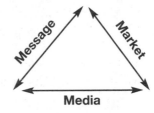

The No B.S. Rules

I'll lay the foundation first. (A radical idea itself!) Please copy these and post them somewhere where you'll see them often until you get them memorized. Doing so will keep you on track, save you a lot of money, and dramatically improve your marketing.

From now on, every ad you run, every flyer you distribute, every postcard or letter you mail, every web site you put up, every/anything you do MUST adhere to these rules. To be fair, they are simplistic and dogmatic, and there are reasons to violate them in certain situations. But for now, sticking to them as a rigid diet will work. You can experiment later, after you've first cleansed your business of toxins.

Rule 1.   There Will Always Be an Offer or Offer(s)

Rule 2.   There Will Be a Reason to Respond Right Now

Rule 3.   There Will Be Clear Instructions on How to Respond

Rule 4.   There Will Be Tracking and Measurement

Rule 5.   Whatever Brand Building Occurs Will Be a Happy By-Product, Not Bought

Rule 6.   There Will Be Follow-Up

Rule 7.   There Will Be Strong Sales Copy, Not Vague
          Hyperbole

Rule 8.   In General, It Will Look Like "Mail-Order
          Advertising"

Rule 9.   Results Rule, Period

Rule 10. You Will Be a Tough-Minded Disciplinarian and
          Keep Your Business on a Strict DIRECT Marketing
          Diet for at Least Six Months

I'll briefly go through each of these rules in the next chapter.

CHAPTER 2

The Rules

I once wrote an entire book about breaking rules, and generally speaking, I think rules are for other, ordinary mortals—certainly not for me, and not for you either if you are a true entrepreneur. So you'll chafe at rules here just as I would. However, when you are attempting to un-do bad habits and replace them with new ones, some hard and fast rules are necessary, temporarily. Once you fully understand these and have lived with them for a reasonable length of time, then feel free to experiment if you wish. But get good at coloring inside the lines before ignoring them altogether.

Rule 1
There Will ALWAYS be an Offer or Offer(s).

My old speaking colleague Zig Ziglar always described salespeople who wimped out at the close as "professional visitors," not professional salespeople. From now on, you will be doing selling in print, selling with media, and you rarely want to be just a professional visitor—and in those rare times, only by very deliberate intent, not accident. So, your task is to make a direct-response offer, which fortunately is simple. An offer is something like "Buy this, get a 2nd one free" or "Call for your free catalog and DVD." The more interesting and appealing the offer, the better. But the most important basic point is: never end a "conversation" in any media without making a direct offer.

Go check your Yellow Pages ad. Odds are, no offer. A lot of businesses even run newspaper ads with no offers! They have what's called an implied offer. The ad for the funeral home, for example, gives its name, years in business, hours, and facts about services it offers. The implied offer is: when you need us, we'll bury you. A lot of businesses run this same kind of ad: Here we are; here's what we do. Stop doing this. It's stupid. To finish the example of the funeral home, you can run the same ad, but add the following:

For a free "Pre-Need Planning Kit" and Audio CD, *19 Financial and Estate Planning Tips for Responsible Family Leaders*, call our free recorded message anytime at (000) 000-0000. It will be sent by mail, no cost, no obligation.

If you want two offers, you can add:

"Tour our new Lakeside Eternal Rest Gardens, get answers to any questions you have about pre-need planning, by appointment, Monday–Saturday. Call William Tourguide at (000) 000-0000. Free Thank-You Gift when you visit: complimentary dinner for two at The Golden Corral Steakhouse."

So, be firm about this. Nothing, I mean nothing, goes out your door without offers.

Rule 2
There Will Be Reason to Respond Right Now

My friend, top direct-response copywriter John Carlton, always advises imagining your prospective customer or client as a gigantic somnambulant sloth, spread out on the couch, loathe to move his sleeping bulk, phone just out of reach. Your offer must force and compel him to move now. Your goal is immediate response. A plain vanilla, dull, mundane offer won't do it.

Rule 3
Clear Instructions

Two subrules: One, confused consumers do nothing. Two, most people do a pretty good job of following directions. Most marketers' failures and disappointments result from giving confusing directions or no directions at all.

When you put together any marketing tool—ad, flier, sales letter, web site, phone script, etc.—it should be a single, focused path with high sidewalls (to prevent the prospect from wandering off), that leads to a point of decision and action. At that point, you must tell the prospect exactly what you want him to do next, how and when, and what will happen as soon as he does.

Stop sending out anything absent such clear instructions.

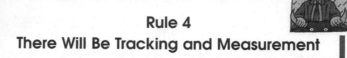

Rule 4
There Will Be Tracking and Measurement

You need real, hard facts and data to make good, intelligent marketing decisions. Making such decisions based on what you or your employees think is happening, feel, guess, have a sense of, etc. is stupid. And you don't want to be stupid, do you?

Tracking means accurately collecting all the information you need to determine what advertising is working and what isn't, which offer is pulling and which isn't, what marketing has traction and what doesn't. Tracking leads to knowing what your return on investment is for each dollar.

Admittedly, it can be a bit tricky. For example, Ad #1 may pull in new customers at $122.80 in cost and Ad #2 at $210.00, so you might decide Ad #1 is the winner. Ah, but the average purchase amount of those coming in from Ad #2 is $380.00; the average from Ad #1 only $198.00. Now which is better? Further, 30% of those from Ad #2 may return and buy again within 30 days, from Ad #1, only 8%. Now which is better? Don't you dare shrug this off as too complicated. Think. Set up systems to capture the data you need; set aside time to do the necessary analysis. If it's painful and confusing at first, it'll get easier. It will prove profitable.

Employees can often be an obstacle to accurate tracking: sometimes out of laziness, sometimes stubbornness, sometimes for more Machiavellian motives, such as concealing their own negligence or incompetence. If there's been no tracking, there will be resistance to it. So, give clear, simple, firm instructions about what is required. Then, if need be, follow the old Oakland Raiders' tough guy Howie Long's plan for parenting a teenage girl: "First boy who shows up, I'll shoot him. I figure the word will get around." Firing can continue until compliance occurs. I'm amazed and amused every time I hear a business owner say "my employees won't do that." Well, who's working for whom?

From now on, ye shall spend no dollar without tracking the ROI.

Rule 5
Branding as By-Product

Traditional brand-building is fine for giant companies with huge budgets vying for store shelf space and consumers' recognition. If you are the CEO of Heinz or Coors or some company like that, playing with other peoples' marbles, by all means buy brand identity. Have fun. But if you are an entrepreneur invest-ing your own marbles, then forget all about it. Focus on response and sales. If you develop brand recognition acciden-tally along the way, great. But do not spend even a dime solely and exclusively on creating it. Do not let trying to get it inter-fere with response.

As example, there are many types of direct-response lead generation ads, designed to motivate a qualified prospect for a particular product or service to step forward, identify himself, and ask for information, that work much better "blind," absent any company name or logo, than they do with identity dis-closed. One version is the now classic Warning-type ad: "Warning to Mutual Fund Investors: Expert predicts dramatic change in next 29 days. Information you must have that bro-kers don't want you to know. For free information, call the Fund Investor Hotline at 1-800-000-0000." You kill that ad's response with a big, fat logo and financial planning firm's name and happy slogan in it. When such a choice must be made, always choose response and cheerfully sacrifice brand-building.

Brand-building is for very, very patient people with very, very deep pockets. That's probably not you.

Rule 6
There Will Be Follow-Up

I hate waste.

People read your ad, call your place of business, ask a ques-tion, the receptionist answers it, and that's it—no capture of the caller's name, address, e-mail, etc. and no offer to immediately send a free report, gift, coupons. That is criminal waste. It cost money to get that call. Doing nothing with it is exactly the same as flushing money down the toilet. Please go and do so, right now, so you internalize the feeling. Take the largest bill you have in your wallet—a $10, a $20, preferably a $100—go to your toilet, tear it in hunks, let them flutter into the toilet, and flush. You probably won't like it. Good. Remember how much you don't like it every time you fail to follow-up (a lot) on a lead or customer.

Other waste includes no instant follow-up to get a first-time customer back. No follow-up on leads from a trade or consumer show. No follow-up on referrals. When Betty says, "I told Billy Bob about you," you don't just say thanks; you ask for and get Billy Bob's address. You send a nice letter mentioning Betty's recommendation and enclosing coupons, literature, or a gift. Then you send Billy Bob a second letter if he fails to respond. And a third, fourth, and fifth. And put him on your newsletter mailing list for 12 months to forever. That's follow-up.

From now on, nothing you do will be just one thing. There will be a planned sequence of things completed. Any contact by you with a prospect or any contact with you by a prospect will trigger a series of follow-up steps.

Rule 7
There Will Be Strong Copy

Sales and subtlety rarely go hand in hand. There is enormous, overwhelming competition for attention and clutter everyone must cut through. You can't send a shy, timid Casper Milktoast guy out into the street to knock on a door of a home or walk into a business and beg in nearly a whisper for a few minutes of the prospect's time. So you can't do that with ad, flier, letter, or post-card either. Send Arnold Schwarzenegger instead. He'll walk through the door. Be a commanding presence. He shows up, guy drops what he's doing and pays attention.

Lots of the examples in this book and in the linked, free e-mail course provide examples of very strong sales copy. Pay attention! Emulate examples like these, and I urge reading my book, *The Ultimate Sales Letter*.

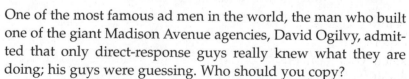

Rule 8
In General, It Will Look Like Mail-Order Advertising

One of the most famous ad men in the world, the man who built one of the giant Madison Avenue agencies, David Ogilvy, admit-ted that only direct-response guys really knew what they are doing; his guys were guessing. Who should you copy?

Any and all ads for any business should mimic mail-order ads. I want you to get your hands on, and study everything as if your life depended on it, you can find written and published by the following short list of people:

- E. Joseph Cossman
- Gerardo Joffee
- Robert Collier
- Joe Sugarman

And also study Bill Glazer because he is a "master" at using mail-order style advertising for bricks 'n' mortar businesses that any of the people I just listed would applaud.

Accumulate a file of full-page mail-order newspaper and magazine ads that are mail-order ads, that ask you to buy or at least request free information, or have a coupon or a toll-free number. Whenever you prepare or approve your ads, flyers, sales letters, or web sites, get out this file and compare. Yours better look like the ones in the file.

Rule 9
Results Rule, Period

A lot of what you see in the remainder of this book may look or feel wrong to you, too bold, too aggressive, too hype-y, too unprofessional, too whatever. Of course, that's the old you reacting to it, before you became a direct marketing pro. But, regardless of your experience in your business or even your expertise as a direct marketer, your opinions and feelings about your marketing don't count. You get no vote because you don't put money into your cash register. Your spouse, momma, neighbor, golfing buddy, competitor or employee don't get to vote either, for the same reason. Plus, they quite probably know zip about direct marketing. The only votes that get counted are the customers' or clients', and the only bona fide ballots are their checks or credit cards. Everything else is hot air. From now on, you will be the most results-oriented businessperson on the planet, immune to opinion, criticism, or guesswork. If it sells, it's good. If it doesn't, it isn't.

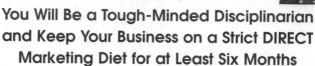

Rule 10
You Will Be a Tough-Minded Disciplinarian and Keep Your Business on a Strict DIRECT Marketing Diet for at Least Six Months

If you go on a diet, there are some things you need to do. First, purge your refrigerator and cupboards of fattening and junk foods. And keep them free of them. Celery sticks, not cookies. Second, decide on an eating plan and stick to it patiently and persistently. Third, get some tools, like a scale. Fourth, count something—calories, fat grams, carbs, Weight Watchers points, something—so you can subtract by the numbers, manage with numbers. Fourth, step up your exercise.

Same thing with your transformation to lean, mean direct marketer. First, purge your business of junk—pretty brochures that violate most or all of the above rules. Dead ads that just lay there. Gentle, subtle, boring sales letters. Uncooperative staff. Out with the old, in with the new. Second, decide on a marketing plan. I suggest my book *The Ultimate Marketing Plan* as a helpful tool. Third, get some tools, like new ads, fliers, coupons, sales letters, web sites, and scripts for handling incoming calls. Fourth, count. See Rule 4, There Will Be Tracking and Measurement. Fifth, mentally exercise. Start reading books and articles, listening to recordings, and going to seminars about direct marketing.

You need to be very careful not to let anything into your new direct marketing world that doesn't belong there. Consider the bread the restaurant gives me with my salad. As often as once a week, I get a big Caesar salad with grilled chicken from a nearby restaurant as takeout. They always put one-third of a loaf of fresh baked bread in the bag with it, even though I ask them not to. When I get home, I take the bread out, take it out of its wrapper and throw it in the big garbage can in the garage before entering the house. Why? Because I have a whole lot less discipline than most people give me credit for. If that bread gets past the perimeter into my house, I'll eat it. So I can't let it in. You've got to do the same thing with your business. Anything that doesn't conform to the prior nine rules, do not let it in at all. Just say no. And bar the door.

CHAPTER 3

The Results Triangle

*E*very marketing system I've ever devised for any client — and they now number in the hundreds and hundreds, commanding fees exceeding $100,000.00 and royalties far larger for many—every one has been based on this Triangle.

There are three components to marketing—for anything, anywhere, at any time, at any price, to anyone, under any conditions. Every individual loves to insist his business circumstances are somehow different. Not so. Every business on earth, past or present, requires these three things to prosper.

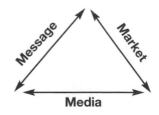

They are not in sequential order, because they can't be. One is no more important than the other. One does not necessarily precede the other, although in the following three chapters I've dealt with them in my preferred order. But you need all three in place simultaneously. Think of it as a three-legged stool. It can't stand with any one leg broken or missing. It needs all three.

It is also a closed triangle. Each of the three components feeds the other two. If you will, "marketing energy" flows laterally, to and from each component, to and from the other two.

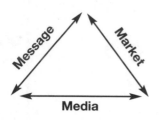

It is a simple visual to remember, but if you would like a coffee mug with the triangle on it, all you need to do is take the time to send five strong, personal letters, faxes, or e-mails to businesspeople who know and respect you, recommending they buy and read this book. Then, send me copies of the five letters, along with your own comments about this book. (A sample appears in Figure 3.1 for your convenience.) Also send a shipping label made out to you. I'll send you a coffee mug as a gift. Send everything to: Dan Kennedy, Kennedy Inner Circle, Inc., 5818 N. 7th Street, #103, Phoenix, Arizona 85014. Sorry, but the offer expires in December 2006.

There are quite a few ways to screw up the Triangle:

Right Message—Wrong Market—Right Media

Right Message—Right Market—Wrong Media

Right Message—Wrong Market—Wrong Media

Wrong Message—Right Market—Right Media

Wrong Message—Wrong Market—Right Media

Wrong Message—Right Market—Wrong Media

Wrong Message—Wrong Market—Wrong Media (the trifecta)

There's only one way to get it right.

Right Message—Right Market—Right Media

FIGURE 3.1: Sample Letter

From: _____

Dear _____:

I just finished one of THE best books on marketing I have ever read, and I thought you would want to know about. It's going to change a lot of what I do for the better, and I bet you'd want to act on its suggestions, too.

The book is Dan Kennedy's *No B.S. Direct Marketing for NON-Direct Marketing Businesses*—and "no b.s." it is!

You can get it at any bookstore or online bookseller, or at least get information about it free at www.nobsbooks.com.

Oh, and it comes with an Audio CD by the author that's fantastic.

You can thank me later. Get the book now!

_____

CHAPTER 4

Markets

With a nod to Dr. Seuss: the WHO is very, very important
When you choose and use media, WHO are you hunting for?

When you craft your Message, WHO is it supposed to resonate with?

Sadly, most businesspeople cannot accurately and completely describe exactly WHO they want to respond, WHO is their ideal customer, WHO is their current customer. And for the most part, they are running about playing a marketing version of Blind Archery. A dangerous game.

I have dealt with many, many, many examples of this over the years. Let me tell you about three that are instructive and, although in very, very different businesses, reveal the same very powerful, profitable, pretty much secret principle.

Scenario 1. A member of one of my coaching groups owned a very profitable, very unusual business: for a fee, his company helped frustrated U.S. men meet and marry brides from foreign countries and arranged for their brides' immigration. His was a one-stop shop, providing access to thousands of prescreened women in Russia, Asia, and other lands eager to marry U.S. men. It facilitated communication, coaching, trips to the different countries, and assistance with legal matters. The basic fees were $495.00 to $995.00 when he joined my group, but they quickly leapt to $4,995.00 to $9,995.00 on my advice, with no change in client acceptance, although that's not my point here. I questioned him about the WHO of his business. Who were the clients? Who were the best clients? He told me they were everybody: preachers, teachers, truck drivers, pro golfers, executives, barbers, butchers, and candlestick makers. But when I asked if there were more of one than the other, I hit the nerve; he didn't know. So we investigated. And we found that about half of all the clients were twice divorced, long-haul truck drivers. Now I want you to think about what use we might make of that piece of information, and I'll return to it a bit later.

Scenario 2. A client sells a home-based business opportunity aimed at "white collar" men and women. He advertised in *USA Today*, newspapers, and business opportunity magazines, like *Entrepreneur*. Again, I inquired about the WHO. His buyers included "all kinds of" sales professionals, accountants, lawyers, doctors, executives, and retired persons. But when I asked if there were more of one than the other, he wasn't sure.

We investigated. Over one third were accountants and CPAs. About one third mortgage brokers, and the remaining one third a mixed bag. Now I want you to think about what use we might make of that piece of information, and I'll return to it a bit later.

Scenario 3. I was doing a lot of work with a particular chiropractor. We meticulously analyzed his records and surveyed his patients, to discover two things: the majority of his fee for service, cash patients had two things in common: One, they paid using their American Express cards, rather than VISA or MasterCard, and two, they subscribed to *Prevention* magazine. The majority. Now I want you to think about what use we might make of that piece of information, and I'll return to it a bit later.

Go back to the first example, the foreign brides business. With the information uncovered, here's what he could do: first, radically alter the places he advertised and the amounts of money allocated to different places. There are magazines for and read only by truck drivers, truck stops where literature can be distributed, mailing lists, even phone number lists that can be "voice broadcast" messages. (See Chapter 16, How to Automate Your Marketing.) So instead of spending 100% of the ad dollars in general media like *USA Today*, at least half should go where half the clients are coming from. In the Kennedy Marketing Triangle, I've just addressed Media. Second, he could take all his generic ads, sales letters, testimonial booklets, etc. and tweak them, creating a version talking only to and about truck drivers, featuring only testimonials from truck drivers. In the Triangle, that's Message.

Consider the second example—obvious now, isn't it? There are magazines for and read only by accountants and CPAs, mailing lists, associations, meetings, and conferences. Same kind of Media change, same kind of Message change.

Now, the third example. In the commercial mailing list marketplace, you can rent the list of *Prevention* magazine subscribers by zip code (as well as by gender, age, etc.), and you can rent the list of American Express cardholders by zip code. He took only the duplicates, the people in his market area on both lists. Because he had to rent 5,000 names from each list as a required minimum, it cost him about $700.00. He only found 27 prime names in his area—a cost of about $26.00 to find each. A lot of business owners would scream, "Too much money!" Dumb, dumb, dumb. How much do you think it will cost to run ordinary ads or mass mail neighborhoods to find 27 who precisely and perfectly match your ideal customer profile? From sequential mailings to the 27, he got 11 into the office (a 40% response *vs.* 1% or 2% norm from mass mail); 9 became patients, producing $17,800.00 in immediate revenue, plus long-term value, plus referrals. That's the potential power of laser beam targeted marketing.

All three scenarios teach the same lessons. The WHO is very, very important. If you know WHO you want to attract, you can often find media or lists that reach only them. Often, the right description of WHO already exists in your business, and you just haven't paid any attention to it or thought about how to use it.

Well, what if you're new in business and have no backlog of data about your WHO? Try common sense. Maybe check your trade association or even competitors for some clues to WHO. A client of mine starting a brand new, high-end, gourmet food and wine store camped out in a competing store's parking lot and a near-by top-price restaurant's parking lot, stick counted make and model of cars, and found a profound bias for new and nearly new foreign luxury cars, so he rented lists of those car owners in his zip code. Or, at least, start out with your own preferences. WHO do you want as client or customer? One way or another, get out of the anybody 'n' everybody place at your earliest opportunity.

Personally, I long ago discovered that my best clients, best coaching group members, and highest value customers are politically conservative males from everywhere but the East Coast "blue states." Are there exceptions? Yes, and in sizeable numbers—I have and have had great women clients, a few flaming liberal clients, and very good clients from New York. But the majority are conservative males, mostly from the midwest, south and southwest. Consequently, I make no attempt to be all-inclusive in what I write, say, or produce, nor do I give even a minute's thought to whom I might offend in the lower-value, lower-percentage groups. I know my prime Market, and I design my Messages and choose my Media accordingly.

At bare minimum, let this chapter make you think more about Markets. Too many businesspeople think about themselves, their products, their services, and what they want to say about all that, rather than thinking about WHO is likely to be hungriest, most eager, and most receptive and is readily and affordably reachable that they'll enjoy doing business with.

CHAPTER 5

Message

I f you want a yard full of deer, do not put a 50-pound block of cheddar cheese outside. Put a big salt block. If you want rats and mice, try the cheese. If you want to catch trout, do not tie an old shoe to your fishing line. Very simple formula:

Match Bait to Critter

Once you pick the critter you want to attract, as we just discussed in the previous chapter, you can then pick or create the right bait. In marketing, "bait" means two things: your Message and whatever "thing" you offer to spark direct response, whether that's literature and information, a free service, or a gift of one kind or another.

Most businesspeople get poor results for their advertising and marketing because they put out no bait, lousy bait, or the wrong bait for the critters they hope to attract.

No bait, that's ordinary image or brand advertising, rather than direct response advertising.

Lousy bait is boring, uninteresting, unappealing bait. A free report on "How to Buy Insurance" is lousy bait. A free report on "How to Legally Avoid all Estate Taxes" might be better bait—for the right critter. That free report combined with a free audio CD with an interview with five wealthy executives about tax planning mistakes they were making and how they fixed them and another free report "How to Double Tax Free Yield on IRA, SEP, Keogh and other Retirement Funds" makes for better bait.

Wrong bait for wrong critters—the free report on estate taxes if you want to attract young married couples.

Sure, this (now) seems incredibly obvious and elementary. Yet 90% of all advertising features one of these three bait mistakes.

Then, there's a bigger issue on how this bait thing fits in. It's called Message-to-Market Match (or mis-match). Most business marketing is generic, one size fits all. Most marketing is done with generic tools: one brochure, one catalog, one web site for everybody. But one size never fits all. What's magnetic is a Message just for me! As soon as I see it, I jump out of my skin because it is clearly for me, about me, and matches me and my pain, fear, passion, hopes.

CHAPTER 6

Media

The list of media choices is longer than all the pages of this book ripped apart and laid end to end.

There are newspapers, magazines, free standing inserts, TV, radio, coupons, postcards, fliers, sales letters, catalogs, web sites, e-mail, faxes, telemarketing, billboards, vehicle signs, bus bench signs, skywriting, package inserts, imprinted golf tees, and web site addresses tattooed on boxers' heads or strippers' body parts, and thousands of variations and other choices. What's good? What's bad? What's best? What's worst?

No simple answer. Sorry.

First, it varies a lot by business. But more importantly, it has to do with WHO you are trying to reach. Do they pay attention to and respond to the media? A flier for two-for-one pizza stuffed under windshield wipers of cars at a swap meet may be a good media. A flier about investing at least $250,000.00 in international currency funds stuffed under the same windshield wipers, bad media. But it's not the media. It's the use of it. The one sure thing is this: if the media can't be used to deliver a *direct response* message, skip it.

With that said, your mandate is to try to find ways to use as many different media as you possibly can. Most business owners become lazily dependent on only one, two, or three means of getting customers, leaving themselves vulnerable to sudden business disruptions and entry of more aggressive competition.

CHAPTER 7

Mastery

L et this book be the stimulus for you to master direct marketing.

Early in life, I heard Earl Nightingale, one of the great success education authors, speakers, and broadcasters, suggest that with as little as one dedicated hour a day, you could become a world class expert in just about anything in a year to no more than three years. I took him seriously. I am a 100% self-educated direct-marketing expert. No college, no apprenticeship. Just a study of everything I could get my hands on and diligent application.

Of course, you may not aspire to a career as an expert for hire. Probably not. However, the breakthrough realization for you is that *you are in the marketing business.* You are *not* in the dry cleaning or restaurant or widget manufacturing or wedding planning or industrial chemicals business. You are in the business of *marketing* dry cleaning services or restaurants or widgets or wedding planning or chemicals. When you embrace this, it makes perfect sense to set your sights on marketing mastery. If you are going to make something your life's work and chief activity and responsibility, why not do it exceptionally well?

You will find a common thread throughout the individual chapters in Section II. If you look for it, you will find it. It is the golden key not just to more sales or profits, or to less waste in advertising, or to more money in the bank—it is the golden key to much more, to things much more important. Please look for this as you read these chapters. If you find it and correctly identify it, it should motivate you to act on my next piece of advice.

The very best, most profitable, most life-changing program you could put yourself on for the next 6 to 12 months is devoting one solid, uninterrupted, inviolate hour each and every day to mastering direct marketing. If you follow all my recommendations, get your hands on all the resources I suggest, do the things I'm going to advise, you'll not only invest those 180 to 365 hours, but also invest about $25,000.00. It'll be the best time and money you've ever spent. The complete list of recommended reading, home study courses, other resources, seminars, etc. is included in the free e-mail course linked to this book, available at www.nobs books.com.

Keep this firmly in mind as you proceed through this book: most business owners are enslaved by their businesses, not masters of them. They find themselves working for their businesses, rather than owners of businesses working for them. There is a key to turning this back around, as it should be. You can find it here. Then you can truly be the master of your business life.

Inside NON-Direct Marketing Businesses Successfully Using Direct Marketing

Retail Businesses

The following two chapters, by Bill Glazer and Chauncey Hutter, Jr., present strategies and examples for applying direct marketing to retail stores and retail service businesses.

If you need to get your customers to come to your store, showroom or office, preferably at a particular time—on demand—and for particular reasons, then these two chapters are for you.

CHAPTER 8

How Outrageous Advertising Turns Ordinary Retail Stores into Super-Profitable Marketing Businesses
Bill Glazer

Today, I'm known throughout seven different retail industries, and many others, as an "expert" in what I call Outrageous Advertising. But I started in retail doing business much like all other retailers. My odyssey contains many lessons that can be profitable for any business owner.

Retail Is in My Blood

My father started our family-owned menswear retail business in downtown Baltimore, Maryland, in 1946, and I grew up working in the store. Started selling suits at the ripe old age of 12. Joined the business "full time" after graduating from college in 1974.

At that time, there were a total of 14 menswear stores just in downtown Baltimore, and four department stores selling menswear as well. But, in the 1980s, I noticed something very interesting happening to my industry. Stores began to close at a rapid rate, and although we were doing okay, I was obviously concerned about our future.

So, I Decided to Become a Student

At first, I was a student of the menswear industry. Went to all the menswear industry seminars. Studied how other menswear stores were operating their businesses. Read whatever books there were about retailing, and I finally noticed something of significant value.

I noticed that most of the remaining menswear stores were basically doing the same thing that I was doing at the time, which was studying what everyone in our niche was doing and then basically copying it. Or in other words, we were all copying everything that wasn't working.

To Make Matters Worse

By observation, I noticed that retailers were spending most of their time on the merchandising and operations of their businesses and almost no time on the third key component, which was just as important. Of course, that's marketing.

Perhaps it was ignored because the marketing that they attempted was ineffective and costing them a lot of money. Whatever the reason, most retailers did not understand the overall importance of marketing and the effect it could have on their businesses.

I Went Outside of My Own Industry

I began to study the marketing of successful businesses. I spent a fortune with top experts and consultants like Dan Kennedy. I took all of this cutting-edge marketing information and applied it to my own business with almost frightening effectiveness.

In fact, I saw big results immediately and within just two years, my two menswear stores grew to become the two most successful menswear stores in all of Maryland. In fact, in spite of the BIG BOX chains doing their best to crush us, my stores KEPT all of our customers and INCREASED sales. (Last year alone, we did 253% *better* than the national average for stores our size.)

What's perhaps more important is that I then discovered that the SYSTEM that I developed for my own stores works for *every* other kind of retail business you can think of. In fact, I currently have over 3,100 retailers using my strategies in just about every category of retail, including apparel, jewelry, furniture, gift shops, sporting goods, bicycle shops, outdoor stores . . . you name it.

What's more, my SYSTEM of proven marketing tactics works just as amazingly well in New York City or San Diego as it does in Virginia City, Nevada, (population 700) or any other small town. It works whether a retailer owns one store and wears several different hats right or operates 50 store chains. Best of all, it works regardless of what's going on with the economy.

I'm Humbled by All of the Notoriety

In 2000, the industry journal *MR Magazine* named "Bill Glazer's Retail Business Building Marketing System" to the list of the 100 Top People, Places, and Things Impacting the Industry at the

Millennium . . . the equivalent of being named to *People* or *Time* magazine's list of 100 most noteworthy or influential individuals. I have been featured in various prestigious marketing and business magazines, including *Direct Marketing News* and *Entrepreneur.*

The Maryland Small Business Administration selected me as one of the top two "Business People of the Year." Imagine that. They gave the award to . . . of all people . . . a retailer. That same year, I won the prestigious RAC Award at the 2002 Retail Advertising Conference. This honor is equivalent in retail to an Oscar in movies or to an Emmy in television. Imagine an independent retailer competing and winning against giants like Target, Wal-Mart, Chevrolet, Best Buy, and Payless Shoe Source.

Sounds incredible . . . an "independent retailer" with two menswear stores in Baltimore, beating out the Big Boys with *smarter* and *cost-effective* marketing and helping thousands of other "independent" retailers do the same thing.

Perhaps the shining jewel of my accomplishments was when Dan Kennedy, America's top marketing guru, recently said of me:

> As you might imagine, given my extensive travels, speaking to over 200,000 businesspeople a year for ten consecutive years, I've seen the advertising and marketing of hundreds and hundreds of retailers and nobody, and I mean nobody, has a handle on direct-response advertising and marketing for retail business like Bill Glazer.

How Can this Be? What Are My Secrets?

I'm not sure I have any real secrets, I just *test,* then *teach* emotional direct response marketing where business people can see and measure a *significant* return on their investments.

For example, there's a retailer who owns a lingerie shop in Chevy Chase, Maryland, who used one of the templates for "dirt cheap" postcards and reported a 20% jump in sales for the month with my Anniversary promotion.

Although I teach dozens of different promotions like the one described above, what I have found is that what all business people really need is a fully integrated system. So in addition to promotions, there also needs to be a strong basic foundation such as a customer reactivation program, a referral program, and free publicity campaigns.

Now I also deliver a completely "done-for-you" Customer Loyalty Program that automatically triggers mailings to be sent out without the retailer having to lift a finger. Results are truly outstanding, and it is not uncommon to get reports like we do from a gift shop owner in Colony, Texas, who has tracked twice as many visits to her store from customers enrolled in the program and best of all . . . they spend four times as much per year.

Lately, I've really embraced the new frontier of low-cost media, which is, of course, e-mail marketing. I teach my members to send out e-mails to their customers every week using a specific approach that not only gets the e-mail opened . . . but more importantly, READ!

Two Examples of Outrageous Advertising

I am best known for being somewhat outrageous in my advertising. Whether it is leaving a prerecorded message on over 10,000 customers' home answering machines from an Elvis impersonator, mailing out a diner placemat (Figure 8.1), or sending a five-page, "handwritten" sales letter on yellow legal pad paper (Figure 8.2).

These two examples demonstrate many important things.

First, obviously, they look very different from most direct-mail pieces. In fact, they look odd. The placemat mailing is made to look like a real diner's placemat on one side, then a handwritten sales letter from me is on its back. It's folded up and mailed with a simple address label, and real stamp, as if I had written out, slapped on the label and mailed a real placemat. Because it would be so odd for me to send you a note scribbled on a place mat, you read it—and that's the point! The legal pad letter uses an almost identical idea: a hastily handwritten note from me on legal pad paper. It even has four hand-drawn coupons. This legal pad mailing was also turned into a very successful newspaper ad.

Second, these pieces present very specific offers with deadlines. You shouldn't miss that point.

Third, they trade on my "personal" relationship with my customers, even though there are tens of thousands of them. I communicate with them all the time, person to person. I send Thanksgiving cards, I send voice broadcasts that sound as if I called and left a message on their answering machines or voice mail, I send picture postcards when I travel. We don't communicate much as a company. I communicate as a person.

Finally, getting mailings from me or seeing my ads in the newspaper is fun. My customers look forward to getting my mail, to see what outrageous thing I'm doing now!

Bill Glazer is the number-one most celebrated marketing advisor to the retail industry, with thousands of top stores

worldwide utilizing his innovative direct-response advertising and direct mail, lab tested with his own two exceptionally successful Baltimore stores. For a FREE copy of his report How to Simply and Easily Discover the Hidden Wealth Buried in Your Business *visit his web site at www.bgsmarketing.com, or call (800) 228-8178, press extension 3, and leave your name and address.*

FIGURE 8.1: Bill Glazer's "Diner Placemat" Outrageous Advertising Mailing

This is a great example of one of Bill Glazer's outrageous advertising mailings. He created a diner placemat, complete with a simulated coffee stain, with a sales letter on the back.

FIGURE 8.2: Bill Glazer's Five-Page, Handwritten Sales Letter

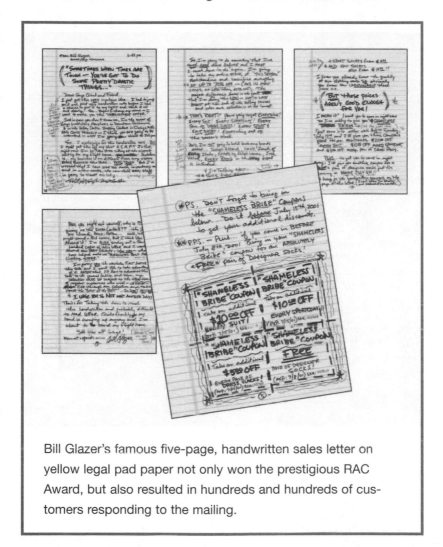

Bill Glazer's famous five-page, handwritten sales letter on yellow legal pad paper not only won the prestigious RAC Award, but also resulted in hundreds and hundreds of customers responding to the mailing.

CHAPTER 9

Who Else Wants to Know How a Guy with NO Tax Experience Took a Two-Room Tax Office Doing $50,000.00 in Sales with a Couple of Seasonal Employees and Built a $4 Million a Year Tax Business with 24 Locations and 440 Employees?

Chauncey Hutter, Jr.

The short answer to this question: DIRECT RESPONSE MARKETING.

The longer answer . . . well, that's what this chapter is all about. You see, to this day I still do NOT know how to prepare my own tax return. (My CPA brother does it for me.) But as you'll soon learn, getting quality leads from proven-to-work marketing campaigns and then closing sales is more important than doing the taxes.

And more specifically, using the power of direct response marketing when testing various promotions to find out what campaigns work well, better, and best . . . then, being able to predict within a reasonable variance what kind of Return On Investment could be expected . . . then, leveraging that information so similar successful results happen in 10 or 20 market areas at the same time instead of just one . . . WILL made a dramatic impact in whatever business you're running!

This kind of impact allowed a small $50,000.00 a year tax office to grow into a $1 million company in just a few short years, and then continue to prosper even more profitably once these successful strategies were systemized for maximum impact.

Let me give you a little background on our tax business so you can understand the full power of using direct response marketing in your business—whether you run a business now or plan on starting a new venture in the future.

As you've already seen, our family-owned, multimillion dollar tax business wasn't always this big. In 1990, I went to work for my father's small, two-room tax business. He was doing about $50,000.00 in sales with a couple of seasonal employees and could not afford to pay me, but he offered me a $200.00 per week draw on whatever I sold. So I went door-to-door selling payroll and bookkeeping services to small businesses. This position was anything but glamorous, especially during the summer I started. Some business owners would feel sorry for me walking around in the August heat, so they'd listen to my pitch out of pity.

I made enough sales to cover the $200.00 a week draw. Then we got to tax season. In January, small business owners were much more receptive to what I had to say because taxes were on their minds. I discovered in a flash whether I had "hot" prospects. The owners' eyes would light up and they would stop whatever they were doing and ask me some tax questions.

Now remember, I didn't then . . . just like I don't today . . . know a thing about taxes. So my answer was always, "I'll get back to you on that—the tax experts are back at my office." But while I was there, I found out more about their businesses and what kind of tax services they wanted.

This process was effective, but it took a long time because it was just me. Manual labor usually is very effective if you are good at what you do. Plus, it is very inexpensive if you don't count your time. And at this point, I did have some time, but not for long.

Discovering What Business We Are Really In

My father had begun to file tax returns electronically the year before so we were getting a good number of calls in January asking about this new, faster, and more accurate service. Because I was the "sales guy," I was delegated to answering the phone. I also greeted people when they came in the door. The other employees would handle filling out tax forms for clients and making sure all the numbers were right before transmitting them to the IRS.

Having a person with sales ability on the phone or face-to-face with clients turned out to be a very good strategy for growth. I didn't realize at the time, but the national brand name tax firms and other competitors were putting their worst tax preparers who "didn't make the cut," or those new employees "lowest on the totem pole," on the phone, almost like a demotion. They believed that TAXES were the most important part of the business and so their "stars" were put in the tax preparing positions.

I knew instinctively that *we needed to MAKE THE SALE first, then we could help them with their taxes*. So if the first contact was over the phone, then I wanted to sell 'em on coming to us vs. the other tax professionals. If being friendly to someone and helping them feel comfortable when they first walk into our office helped with their overall experience and improved referrals, then I wanted to make sure we were doing a great job at this as well.

Needless to say, we got busy! And something very interesting was happening in our office, but I was too green to realize the significance. For every ten people walking through the door at the beginning of the tax season, nine of them were new clients! As I reviewed these numbers at the end of the night, I thought, "Wow!" I had never seen such a high ratio of new clients vs. existing clients coming through the door of an established business.

Well, little did I know, we were about to get flooded with business! The volume was staggering. People crammed into every nook of the office. We "took over" the lobby, the hallways, the front porch, and the whole sidewalk area of our building. Everyone WANTED what we had. We almost immediately had to go to a third shift with employees, who were happy working extra hours.

Offer Services People WANT, Not What they Need

If you missed it, the important part of what I just said was "everyone wanted what we had." You might be thinking that sounds crazy, "Everyone wanted to file their taxes?" Well, not really. Just because we're in the tax business doesn't mean that is the real business we are in. In most cases, *successful business owners are crystal clear on what their REAL business is.* In my case, I'm in the "quick money" business.

Oh, yes, my business does file tax returns for folks. But that's not why people are lining the streets to get in my office. It is because the electronic filing services I offer are exactly what a certain demographic of client wants. Let me briefly explain.

I target the lower income, blue collar families in our market areas. These folks have household annual incomes that range no higher than about $34,000.00. If they meet a few other qualifications, they can receive Earned Income Credits from the government. For some families, these checks can be as high as $6,000.00 or $7,000.00 (average is about $3K), and this money is tax free, going straight into their pockets.

Well, we offer a variety of e-filing services. Most of our clients "need" this earned income credit to help pay bills and buy clothes or whatever is on their lists. In a hypothetical case, the two choices are:

1. Get $5,000.00 mailed to your home in six to eight weeks by government check,

OR

2. Get $1,000.00 bucks in 30 minutes, $3,700 tomorrow and don't worry about paying anything for this service, the fees will be automatically deducted from the refund check. (Our bank vendor loans the money to our client anticipating the IRS will pay them in a couple of weeks. Their refund anticipation loan fees and our e-filing and tax preparation fees are all deducted from the clients' refund check.)

What my clients WANT is QUICK MONEY! Most choose to take as much of their refund check from Uncle Sam as they can, as fast as possible.

You might be thinking, "I would never do that!" (Pay hundreds of dollars to a bank and a tax firm to get only most of my money early instead of just waiting about a month and a half to get all of it.)

Well, guess what—YOU are not my client. And neither am I.

When my father met with the tax software vendor the year before and this whole idea was explained to him, he said the same thing, "Who would pay for this kind of service?" My father reasoned, it would only take two or three people to ask for this kind of "electronic filing bank loan service" to pay for the tax software so what the heck, let's give it a try. (Some 454 clients asked for and received this kind of service the first year, and 1,283 clients in tax season number two.)

I've had CPAs, accountants, and other tax business owners tell me over the years they just didn't see the value in offering a service that didn't make good financial sense to their clients. What I've said to them for years has been, there is a certain profile of individual or family who, no matter what a financial expert says to do, is going to want money immediately.

So if they are going do it anyway (and it is a legal and very legitimate service which millions of people ask for each year), I say, "Go ahead and give 'em what they want," and do so in a way that is head and shoulders better than other tax firms offering similar services. (We offer guarantees on speed, accuracy, customer service, etc.)

HOT BUTTON Benefits Leveraged Through Direct Mail

Back in the early 1990s, I didn't know how to write the most effective form of direct mail—long-form sales copy. Instead, my philosophy was: Put the most important benefits of our e-filing tax services on a postcard, and mail it to people most likely to want these benefits. My thought was that I can't go around door-to-door talking to thousands of people in January when they were getting their W–2s from their employer. It was not physically possible for me to be everywhere at once, especially when we went into three new market areas my second year in the business.

The Hot Button Benefits for lower income families wanting our e-filing services were: (1) Fast Money, (2) Big Refund Check, and (3) No Money Paid Up Front.

So on my little 4-by-6 postcard, I put:

Fast Tax Refunds In One Day—Guaranteed!

All Fees Come Out of Your Big Refund Check,

So No Money Needed to Pay Us Up Front!

$10.00 OFF Refund Loan Tax Services

(Name/Address/Phone)

There wasn't much to this simple little card. *If I was knocking on someone's door and trying to sell them something, this is what I would say. So I put it on a postcard and mailed it.*

[Incidentally, I learned how to "get my foot in the door" and sell stuff door to door to people a few years earlier when I took a (mostly) all-commission sales job out of college selling water conditioning and purifying equipment for the home. This 13-month experience taught me a ton about how to later "sell in print" and helped solidify the benefits of direct response marketing much faster than for the typical guy on the street.]

Now I could do a better sales job in person than this postcard could do, but this postcard could go to 10,000 or 20,000 or 30,000 homes (whatever the market size I wanted to target) in one day! And once my simple little sales piece hit, the phones would ring, and we were off to the races!

Putting this simple sales message in print and then mailing to just those most likely to be interested, all at a certain time of the month when the target group would most likely be coming to a tax business to file their return (when they received their W–2s in January) . . . and then to have the phone ring with just the most interested prospects . . . WOW, this direct mail marketing thing was really turning out to be awesome!

Fast Forward 13 Years . . . How Direct Response Marketing Made Us Millions

Over the years, I have learned much more about the most effective ways to strategically use direct mail. There are many ways to skin a cat, and I believe when you are growing any business (or at least maintaining market share), the business owner should always use multiple forms of direct response marketing.

One of the secrets of our tax businesses success has been the ability to effectively promote multiple media campaigns to the same target audience—all in a condensed time period using direct marketing. All of these campaigns stand alone and are held accountable for their ROI, but the pile on, multiple-media approach inevitably boosts response for all the campaigns.

Look at Figure 9.1, at the end of this chapter.

Now before I give you my million-dollar secrets that took me over a decade to perfect, I'd like to provide a little background.

Remember, I'm targeting low-income families, high school educated with blue collar jobs. (MARKET) This target audience wants the biggest possible tax refund in their hands as fast as possible... and not having to pay for it with-out-of-pocket, up-front money is a huge bonus. (MESSAGE) And finally, the actual form of direct marketing, like a sales letter, newspaper insert, Yellow Page ad, etc. is the vehicle by which the message will be delivered to your target market. (MEDIA)

In Figure 9.1, the media is an insert into a coupon magazine, which happens to be hitting in a geographic area around some of our tax offices in late January. One of the reasons I originally chose to test this kind of ad was because of the amount of sales copy I could get delivered into the home for cheap (shared mail *vs.* direct solo mail).

In this case, the two pages of copy cost me only 6 cents per household. That number is really not that important though. The real number I'm interested in is if I spent $1.00, what will I get in return? That is, what is my ROI?

I'll give you the punch line first: Every time this style ad runs (advertorial) in this type of media, offering that sales message (with the timing of employer W–2s in mind), our tax business will make $3.50 to $1.00 in most markets and as high as $6.50 to $1.00 in a few hot markets.

Either way, I'm very happy to be able to invest some money and then measure an increase coming back as a return.

Dirty little secret. Truth be told, I'd be happy spending a dollar and getting a dollar back with a $1.00 to $1.00 ROI. Why? Because I'm getting a customer for FREE! Most business owners do not look at their promotions this way. They think their promo didn't make any money so they stop running the campaign. Well, I know my numbers, and for every ten customers I get coming through my door (even if I don't make any money on them on the front end), 30 percent will refer friends or family members that same tax season. I also look at the lifetime value of a client. Just viewing one tax season is very shortsighted. If these new customers only stay five years with my tax business, I'll make an average of about $750.00 to $1,000.00 per client from our relationship.

Now, back to the ad in Figure 9.1. The message is clear in the headline, FAST MONEY . . . with a little "IRS Protection" Accuracy Guarantee language to help stop those "tire kickers" in their tracks and get them to read some more.

Another tested and proven headline that works every time (and I could easily replace at the top of the ad in Figure 9.1 and get similar successful results) is . . .

> **Biggest and Fastest Tax Refund Loans Allowed**
> **By the IRS . . . Guaranteed!**

The point is, I'm grabbing attention by making a bold promise and almost forcing them to read on to the subhead or the first sentence, and once I've got them reading, I will not bore them. As you can see from the copy, I write in a conversational language, speaking right to them. It's me talking to them just like if I was on their front porch knocking on their door in the old days.

Before I go any further, I guess I should go ahead and answer the questions you have already asked in your mind. Why so many words? Where's the white space? Don't you believe in logos? Branding your name? Something, 'cause this ad just looks downright ugly!

The short, most important answer to why I promote my tax business like this is:

IT WORKS!

Now, I'll get into more details about why I think this style is better than others. But the bottom line is that it doesn't matter what I think or what you think or what your spouse thinks . . . if your marketing is effective and beats your competition hands down, then the only really good next question is, "How can I do more of this kind of direct marketing ASAP?"

This long copy, advertorial style ad is a mixture of what looks like a real article about a topic people are interested in, but near the bottom of the piece there's an obvious offer to take an action. In this case, the next action step is to call or come by one of our tax offices. And guess what happens to the folks who actually read all of these words? They become very QUALIFIED prospects when they contact us for more info about our services. (Much more so than someone reading a simple 4-by-6 postcard.) They are basically pre-sold before they begin dialing.

Next, the white-space issue . . . this is simple, really. No "white space" ever sold anybody anything! Just because big companies waste their advertising money this way doesn't mean you should, too. They have other agendas related to pleasing board members, image, etc. Results? Nah, that's lower down on their list of priorities. It's a shame, but true.

By contrast, words on a page (salesmanship in print) . . . even lots of words in tiny little type sizes . . . can be very persuasive! There are 100 years worth of very successful examples that prove my point. A wise old direct marketing sales copywriter once said, "The more you tell, the more you sell."

It has been my experience, along with many, many other direct marketing experts, that long-form sales copy—split tested against much shorter copy—outperforms fewer words in almost every case. (There are a few exceptions, but 98 percent of the time, you want to write as long as it takes to make the sale.)

Oh, and one other major benefit for using "ugly" style ads: They stand out and grab attention all by themselves! You talk about getting noticed. Using a long headline, a ton of little type sales copy, and NO COLOR (just black and white) will definitely help you stick out from all the advertising clutter.

Hidden Money-Making Direct Mail Techniques You Might Not Notice

You can see exactly what I'm talking about when reviewing Figure 9.1. But, I'll explain in more detail if you look at Figure 9.2 (also shown at the end of this chapter).

One of my favorite sales letter writing formulas is: PROBLEM, AGITATE, SOLVE. In the ad, I'll talk about how I know about a problem(s) my target audience is having. I'll go into detail explaining the pain involved and really agitate the whole issue. Then, of course, after empathizing with my target customer, I come in on a white horse and save the day by not only offering the solution but also by proving I am the "best" solution and offering a reason to take action now!

Taking a prospect through a sales process in print and then not closing the deal in the end would be sinful! (This happens a lot when novice sales copywriters get started.) *Direct response marketing is all about asking someone to respond in a favorable way* so you either get a lead or a sale as a result. *These responses must be trackable and measurable.* Once you've got some baseline numbers to work with, you can begin testing different variables to see if you can improve on your cost-per-lead or cost-per-sale numbers.

Tracking and measuring does NOT have to be complicated. When I first started out 15 years ago, I literally used a piece of notebook paper and a pencil! Today, I am more sophisticated, but all of the principles are the same. What did I spend on a campaign? How many customers did I get? How much was each "sale" worth? What was my total return on investment?

Look at my "WARNING" Headline in Figure 9.2. This ad hits the streets in many different forms (newspaper insert, coupon card decks . . . even a jumbo postcard with a few minor layout changes).

One big key to this promotion's success is TIMING. I like to run this ad about a week before the April 15th tax filing deadline. The target audience of course is procrastinators. The photo and caption grab attention and help tell the sales story, reinforcing the whole theme of the ad.

When I'm putting together a promotion, I like to keep the theme as simple as possible, sticking with the human emotions most likely to cause someone to respond. In Figure 9.1, you saw a lot of "greed copy". . . and now in Figure 9.2, "fear copy" stands out the most.

Greed and Fear: Two Powerful Motivators Get Your Prospects to Take Action!

Nothing happens in any business unless a sale is made. And if you want to make the most sales, you better find out what your market wants the most, and maybe even more importantly, what is it that keeps them up at night, most likely something or someone they fear or are scared to death of.

Fear of loss might be the most common emotion that causes most every kind of person to take an action they usually wouldn't take, but will now because they don't want to feel the pain associated with whatever the fear is.

So what do you immediately think of when I say the letters . . . "I.R.S."? Did the hair on the back of your neck just stand up? Are you sweating right now? Maybe you just had a negative thought or two. I guarantee you didn't automatically think "happy thoughts" when the Internal Revenue Service came into your brain!

That's why I use FEAR to my advantage. I play into the conversation already going on in the heads of my prospects. It doesn't take much to get people rattled so close to the tax filing deadline IF they have not filed their taxes yet.

But don't forget GREED. We all desire more money to some degree. For some, greed takes over their lives and the pursuit of lots of money really fast overwhelms them. For others, well, yes, of course they want extra money in their pockets, but they are not going to beat someone over the head to get it. However, the idea of additional wealth is very appealing.

I know my target market. And after the holidays when the bills have piled up, my customers want their money. It is almost like a feeding frenzy. A bunch of folks walking around talking about how they are going to spend the extra cash they are going to get in a few weeks when they file their taxes. And because greed plays a factor in how a person is going to make his tax filing decision, as a business owner I better not forget to include this in my ad as a major motivating factor.

Being "Different" Increases Response

We've talked about long-form copy, black and white *vs.* full color, and an advertorial look as opposed to a formal, "professional" look with lots of white space branding approach. But look at both ads in Figures 9.1 and 9.2, and see additional nuances that boost the response of my direct marketing.

First of all, my offer is different than every other tax business. Not only do I extend a special discount for responding by a certain date, *I add "extra bonuses" as additional incentive.* Sometimes a unique T-shirt, other times a tool set or jewelry. There are so many options for finding close-out inventory items online these days. You can buy lots of stuff for $3.00 to $5.00, which have perceived values of $25.00 to $50.00! Any type of customer loves getting extra stuff for free. It sets you apart, and sometimes is the determining factor for doing business with you again.

True confession. We survey our customers annually, and one of the questions we ask is why did you come back to us this year? You would be very surprised how many people mention the "bonus gift" as the reason for their return. Hey, that's OK with me. I'll spend $4.00 on a gift to generate another $175.00 sale any day of the week.

Secondly, I use "odd numbered" discounts to be different as well. Other tax business might offer a $20.00 or $30.00 discount. We'll go with $23.00 or $27.00 off any tax preparation service. I've split tested the odd dollar-off offer, and in most cases the LOWER ODD DOLLAR OFF amount generated more sales.

For example: Two ads running in the same market. One ad uses $23.00 off and the other ad $25.00 off. The ads are the same except for the dollar amounts. In most cases, the $23.00 off ad had a higher ROI. I've done a similar split test with $27.00 off and $30.00 off, and again, in almost every case the lower, odd number won.

Lastly, "The WORLD'S LARGEST _____ " has been a successful line in many other direct marketing businesses, used in a variety of ways. I use this formula with my offer to, again, BE DIFFERENT and stand out from my competition. The World's Largest Tax Service Coupon and The World's Largest Procrastinator's Discount are shown in Figures 9.3 and 9.4. You don't want to overuse this strategy, but you will get a bump in response because it is unusual, not normally seen by your customers or prospects.

Direct Response Marketing: The Best Way to Promote ANY Kind of Business!

The tax business is like most other service businesses. If I can use direct response marketing to effectively build a multimillion dollar company, you can do the same in your business.

And you want to know the funny part? After all of the success we've had building our tax business over the years, do you know that NONE of my competition has even tried to copy our success! If I were in their shoes and I saw a competitor grow at the rate we have, I'd want to find out the successful strategies and use them myself. Well, our ads hit the streets and are obviously very public.

So What's the Moral of this Story?

Go against the grain. Do the opposite of what the norm is in your industry. If you do what everyone else is doing, you'll never get ahead and be at the top of your industry. And you don't have to worry about people stealing your ideas. Most will never have a clue!

Our direct response marketing campaigns are like no other in our industry. We experience outrageous results because we are outrageously different than all of our competition. There IS a lesson there. Don't forget it.

I hope this chapter has opened your eyes to a new way to use a very old and reliable system to make money. Best to you and all of your business endeavors.

Chauncey Hutter, Jr. is the nation's number-one marketing expert specializing in the electronic filing and tax preparation industry.

Mr. Hutter is a success coach and business consultant to the electronic tax filing industry. Schedule permitting, Mr. Hutter charges $800.00 per hour or $4,895.00 per day for personal, one-on-one consulting. For more information about Mr. Hutter's services, go to www.chaunceyhutterjr.com.

Franchising opportunities exist for entrepreneurs interested in modeling the PRO-TAX System (limited territories available). Serious inquires only, go to www.thePROTAXfranchise.com.

Written inquires only, use Real Tax Business Success, 504 Old Lynchburg Rd., Suite 2, Charlottesville, VA 22903, fax (434) 984-1590.

FIGURE 9.1: Chauncey Hutter's "Coupon" Advertisement

"$1,000.00 In 29 Minutes* … The Rest Of Your Tax Refund In 24 Hours* — And An IRS-Protection Accuracy Guarantee That Covers You Like A Blanket!"

PRO-TAX: Home Of The Lightning Fast Tax Refunds….Your Money In A Flash – Guaranteed!

[*Refund Anticipation Loan Checks]

Dear Fast Tax Refund Seeker,

All accountants, CPA's and tax preparers are NOT the same.

Most work with every kind of taxpayer, with every kind of tax issue in the IRS tax code. However …

At PRO-TAX, we specialize in "Instant & Next Day Tax Refund Loans" … helping regular folks who want the biggest and fastest tax refunds back from Uncle Sam - keeping the IRS off your back at the same time!

Why does this matter to you?

Because when hard-working middle to lower income folks with families come into one of my tax offices - they don't want to wait any longer than they have to for their money … and they don't want to wonder if they are missing any deductions or other ways to make their refund check even bigger.

That's why at PRO-TAX, we promise the Biggest & Fastest Tax Refunds Allowed By The IRS - Guaranteed!

I hear from regular folks just like you all the time … "Just give me back ALL the money I'm supposed to get from the IRS (I don't want Uncle Sam keeping any of it) and do it FASTER than any other tax business in town!"

So that's what we do. If you want your hundreds or thousands of refund dollars back as soon as possible - PRO-TAX is the right place for you!

"Your Refund Money In Your Hands In A Flash … GUARANTEED!"

PRO-TAX's Instant Lightning Tax Refund Loans are now available for qualified customers! Receive a $1,000 dollar check in 29 minutes or less - Guaranteed and the rest of your refund money the next day if approved. So once we've finished preparing your tax return and you say "check and see if I qualify for an instant lightning tax refund loan" … we'll know almost instantly if you qualify for $1,000 bucks today … and if so, we'll have your check in your hands faster than Domino's can deliver a pizza!

You want your money NOW … TOMORROW … or BOTH! This year, at PRO-TAX we can get qualified customers their money in less than 29 minutes, the next day or a combination of the two … it'll all depend on what our bank says you qualify for -- So come on in to our office and let's find out what

kind of mini-lottery you've won this year!

No Need To Pay Us Up Front With Money You Don't Have!

If you don't have the money in your pocket to cover the cost of any of our Fast As Lightning Refund and tax services - that's OK. You can either choose the INSTANT LIGHTNING TAX REFUND LOAN ($1,000 bucks in 29 minutes or less) or our NEXT DAY LIGHTNING REFUND LOAN product, which, if you qualify gives you your refund money the NEXT day.

[Hey, sometimes our Bank will loan you up to $7,000 the SAME day if the IRS Service Center is running efficiently. When we transmit your file to the IRS, we'll let you know approximately how long the IRS system is taking that particular day.]

I'm not sure what PRO-TAX Lightning Refund Loan Service you might qualify for. But I DO know we can take all the fees for the service you choose and automatically take them out of your refund check SO YOU DON'T HAVE TO PAY ANY MONEY UP FRONT FOR OUR SERVICES!

This is obviously great news for you since I know money is tight this time of year. So don't worry about how you will have to pay for what you want … concentrate on all the stuff you're gonna buy immediately once the bank has released your money so we can print you a check!

FREE $27.00 OFF Special Discount

The enclosed Special $27.00 OFF Discount is yours FREE and good towards any tax service PRO-TAX provides. The "catch" is you gotta file your tax return before the **deadline date** at the bottom of the coupon. **(February 26, 2005)**

Plus, for folks who want the

fastest way to get their refund check back, filing for any of our Lightning Refund Services -- an **EXTRA BONUS** is waiting for you. This year you'll get our brand new, hot off the press PRO-TAX Lightning Refund T-Shirt! (while supplies last)

What To Do Right Now!

Just call or come down to the PRO-TAX office closest to you and we'll be happy to help you file your taxes this year. Our office hours for most of the tax season are 9:00 am to 7:00 pm Mon. - Fri. and 9:00 am to 2:00 pm on Sat. (If you are coming at the end of the day, call ahead to verify how long we're open. Sometimes it will vary.)

Sincerely,

Chauncey Hutter

Chauncey Hutter, Jr.
President, PRO-TAX

PS: Don't take my word on it - listen to what other people are saying about PRO-TAX

"I'm a single mom. I went to PRO-TAX for a quick refund (loan). They didn't let me down. That money sure came in handy after the holidays. Thanks PRO-TAX for making my life easier!" **Kathy Skaggs**

"I went to PRO-TAX one night and my refund (loan) check was ready the next morning - $3,948.00 was in my pocket in less than 20 hours!" **Nathan Cate**

"PRO-TAX helped me get my refund back... they went the extra mile to help me because my husband was away in the military." **Tomeka & Chris Garland**

"PRO-TAX has saved me lots of mental stress over the last four years. They found an extra $1,171.00 on last year's return and called to advise me. I don't have to worry about the IRS anymore with PRO-TAX's Accuracy Guarantee!" **Rebecca Dempsey**

The World's LARGEST Tax Service Coupon
turn over to back page ➞

FIGURE 9.2: Chauncey Hutter's "Warning" Advertisement

FIGURE 9.3: Chauncey Hutter's "Coupon" Advertisement, page 2

THE WORLD'S <u>LARGEST</u> TAX SERVICE COUPON

"Yes, I Want A Lightning Fast Tax Refund -- PLUS 'IRS-Protected- Accuracy' So I'm Covered Like A Blanket After Filing My Taxes ... Guaranteed!"

www.protax.com

EXTRA BONUS

The <u>Hot</u> <u>New</u> PRO-TAX T-Shirt ...

Not valid with any other offer

Code: 3221

<u>FREE</u> $27.00 OFF DISCOUNT
(expires 2/26/05)

FIGURE 9.4: Chauncey Hutter's "Warning" Advertisement, page 2

THE WORLD'S <u>LARGEST</u> PROCRASTINATOR DISCOUNT!

"<u>Yes, I Have Procrastinated Filing My Taxes This Year</u> ... But I Still Want to Protect Myself from All the New Tax Laws and Get MORE Money Back from Uncle Sam with a Peace-Of-Mind Guarantee that'll Keep Me Sleepin' like a Baby when My Taxes are Filed with the IRS this year!"

www.protax.com

EXTRA <u>BONUS</u>

Charlottesville	Charlottesville
29 North	Downtown
973-5313	**977-0696**
Rio Hill Shopping Center	Near the Ice Park, off Water Street
Between Crutchfield & Subway	Behind Mono Loco (in the yellow house)
Waynesboro	**Staunton**
941-8877	**886-7279**
Willow Oak Plaza	Statler Crossing Shopping Center
Near Ben Franklin	Behind Blockbuster

The <u>Hot New</u> PRO-TAX T-Shirt ...
(while supplies last)

Not valid with any other offer

Code: 3203

 FREE $27.00 OFF DISCOUNT
(expires 4/13/05)

Restaurants

As Rory Fatt points out in the next chapter, restaurants are the most popular and prolific small business in America. Most restaurant owners, like many other types of business owners, get into their businesses because of a passion for the "thing," not for marketing. They often discover that food, ambiance, and service excellence is just not enough to create a thriving business. If you run a restaurant, long to own one, or share the restaurateur's preference for doing the "thing" rather than marketing the business, this chapter is for you.

CHAPTER 10

How to Advertise *Less* for New Customers Yet Double Your Profits
Rory Fatt

To the surprise of most business owners, mass media advertising is usually the least profitable thing they can do to build their businesses. I point the restaurant owners I work with in two other directions: (1) target marketing rather than mass advertising and (2) focusing inward rather than outward.

This chapter is for restaurant owners, but the restaurant is a metaphor for most other kinds of small businesses.

Double Your Restaurant Profits in 119 Days or Less

According to statistics, opening a restaurant is the business that most Americans want to start. This desire stems from two factors.

First, the restaurant industry is the largest private sector employer of people in America, with over 9% of employment directly or indirectly associated with the industry—and many of these employees want to be their own boss. The second factor that contributes to this phenomenon is the attractiveness of the image put forth in the media—that running a restaurant is somewhat similar to the way "Sam," played by Ted Danson, did it in the popular sitcom *Cheers*. The image of the restaurant owner sitting behind the bar, mixing beverages, or walking around talking to guests all day must be too appealing to resist. If you've read this far, chances are you are either in this industry now or know someone involved in it—and you know that the appealing image described above is not the entire reality. You are looking for a way to make significantly more money or have more time off from a restaurant that you or someone you know is involved in.

There has been a dramatic evolution in the restaurant industry over the last decade. There was a time when you could start a restaurant and concentrate on serving good food with reasonably friendly service, and the world would beat a path to your door. The phenomenal growth of the national restaurant chains, along with the fact that many people want to open their own restaurants, means starting a successful restaurant is no longer a guarantee of economic independence. In fact, according to the National Restaurant Association, there are 880,000 restaurants (or foodservice operations) in America. That equates to roughly one restaurant for every 400 citizens. So the odds of creating a successful restaurant without a proven marketing system to bring in new customers and get existing guests to return are heavily stacked against anyone wanting to start his own restaurant. With that much competition, the days of providing a good quality meal and expecting your potential guests to beat a path to your door are long gone because . . . .

Being Good Is Not Good Enough

For many of the independent restaurant owners that seek me out, the reality is remarkably different from the Hollywood image of a restaurateur. Many are very unhappy, even disgusted, with the money they take home from their restaurants and the amount of time and energy they have to expend to get it. Most restaurant owners I meet are doing an outstanding job of operating their restaurants, but they lack the knowledge, skills, savvy, and experience to get guests in the door and keep them coming back. In today's highly competitive restaurant marketplace, every known chain can be within a block or two of your restaurant. The sad truth is that simply being good is not good enough anymore. Even the best restaurant in the world will struggle and suffer, even go broke without a steady flow of new, good customers.

You Can't Make $100,00.000 Doing $10.00 an Hour Work
—RORY FATT

Making big money in the restaurant industry is NOT about making food, dicing carrots, or any of the operational aspects of the restaurant for that matter. It's all about the *MARKETING* of your restaurant. You can fight it and go broke, or you can shift your thinking to embrace this fact enthusiastically and make lots of money.

Consider gravity. We can't see it, but it's a force all around us that keeps us from floating off into space. As a result of gravity,

What
Business Are
You In?

if you hold something in your hands and let it go, it will fall to the ground. It's a natural law of the universe. Gravity doesn't care one bit that you don't like it or even if you know that it exists. It's just like proven marketing principles for your restaurant. They work whether you know about them, use them, or not.

When you do make the giant mental paradigm shift to recognizing that the most valuable use of your time and the one that will be bring you the highest rate of return is the marketing of your restaurant's products or services, you will instantly gain an enormous competitive edge over all the other restaurants in your area, including the chains, so you can start making LIFE CHANGING money.

When it comes to getting new customers, many independent restaurants owners simply do not have the answers. They try to copy the big chains, or worse, their competitors' unsuccessful advertising. They believe the myth that if they do what the big chains do, it will help them get and keep their customers. National chains use what I call "Image" or "Institutional" advertising, which is based on the premise that by making people "Aware" of your restaurant and that it "Exists," potential guests will somehow be excited about coming there. This may work for companies that have very, very, very, large advertising budgets. I mean millions. This may work over the long haul if they can afford to divide the cost over dozens, hundreds, or better yet thousands of units. However if a local, independent restaurant owner engages in this type of image advertising, they will go broke trying to make it work. They just do not have the bankroll or the time to make it work. And trust me, the advertising sales rep who sells you advertising space will not stay awake at night if your ad doesn't get you any new guests. Advertising sales reps are in the business of selling advertising space, not results.

What independent restaurant owners need is measurable marketing that produces results in a cost-effective manner. That is, by definition, direct response marketing. Direct response marketing is designed to pay its own way. It is the *only* type of marketing you should do for a restaurant. It is completely opposite of what the national chains ARE doing.

The two things that all successful independent restaurant owners have in common are a marketing system that can be put on autopilot and a network of other successful restaurant owners that they can connect with and share successful, money-making strategies. I've worked with over 4,013 independent restaurant owners, and I've discovered that those that go from struggling to rapid growth, success, and wealth have used a variety of simple tools and resources. I've summarized these tools and resources in the diagram, Figure 10.1, which appears at the end of this chapter. I use this diagram at many of my $1,997.00 per person boot camps. I call it Rory's Law of Restaurant Wealth.

Focus Your Firepower

Marketing too big, that is, not marketing to a specific group of people, is one of the most common mistakes independent restaurants can make. Once you identify your target market and find out what your potential guests want out of a restaurant, you are one step closer to establishing a successful marketing plan that is specific to YOUR restaurant. Who are your best guests right now? Are they catering customers? Delivery, residential, businesspeople coming for lunch? Where do they live and work? What kind of cars do they drive? Once you are able to answer these questions, it becomes a simple issue of finding more of the same people and communicating with them directly.

One of my clients, Salem Suber from Jasper, Georgia, explains the importance of discovering your target market:

> By using your systematic approach to restaurant marketing I tapped a market just north of my town. This meant that I was between a "starving," more rural market and the city they were used to visiting. Before I used this marketing system, these customers were driving past my town, never even knowing I was here. This is one of the reasons I had such a huge residual impact from ONE ad. I tapped a gusher. Whether you believe it or not, every restaurant has an undiscovered gusher of new guests waiting on them, whether it is filling their dining room or expanding their catering.

Customer or Guest?

A lot of restaurant owners underestimate the value of the relationships they have with their existing guests and the value in being able to market to them. You will always make more money from a continuing relationship than you will from a one-time transaction, and who better to market to but the people that just left your restaurant? Note that I refer to your patrons as guests, not customers. The word *customer* implies a one-time transaction, but a guest in your restaurant, just like in your home, implies someone you want to see again and again, creating a repeat, ongoing relationship. The ability to create and nurture a continuing and profitable relationship with your guests is a HUGE competitive advantage an independent operator has over the national chains. An advantage they MUST capitalize on.

One strategy that I teach all of my clients and actively implement in my own company is mailing out a monthly newsletter to guests. This is a great way to strengthen the relationship with your existing customers, to tell your story, and to involve them in a personal relationship with the restaurant and you the owner. It will allow you to give your guests a reason to return more frequently and give you the advertising space to make them aware of the other services you may provide—catering, takeout, etc.— and add a personal connection. Your newsletter can encourage your guests to take advantage of monthly specials, take part in charity promotions, join referral or reward programs, etc.

For Scott Houmes, of Silverdale, Washington, the results from his restaurant's newsletter were fast and dramatic. He said:

> *The most important thing that I got was my guests began to come back a lot more often. And that's one very good way to boost profits: do more business with the customers who know you and like your place. You grow more profits doing that than you do advertising for new guests.*

Another valuable tool that Scott learned from me is the importance of collecting his customer's birth dates. Considering that birthdays are the number-one dining out occasion, it's an important date to remember. As soon as Scott began to implement this targeted marketing approach, he began to collect this information from his customers and sent them each a birthday card offering them a free meal. The beauty of this concept is that nobody goes out for dinner on his or her birthday alone. In fact, testing shows that for every one free meal that is redeemed, you will get 2.3 guests through your door spending much more heavily than average to partake in the celebration with additional beverages, appetizers, and dessert. Once Scott implemented his birthday program, he found that for every 10 he mails, he brings 4 repeat guests in the door. That's a return on investment that you can take to the bank.

What it comes down to is this: You own your own restaurant, you have developed technical skills, and you do good work. You SHOULD be very well paid, taking home more money than you need EVERY week and investing for future financial security. If you are NOT, then how and when are things going to change for the better in your life?

Rory Fatt, president of Restaurant Marketing Systems, provides advertising and marketing tools, training, seminars, and coaching to over 4,000 independent restaurant owners. To get his special report "How to Double Your Profits in 119 Days or Less" FREE, go to www.myrestaurantcoach.com.

FIGURE 10.1: Rory Fatt's Law of Restaurant Wealth

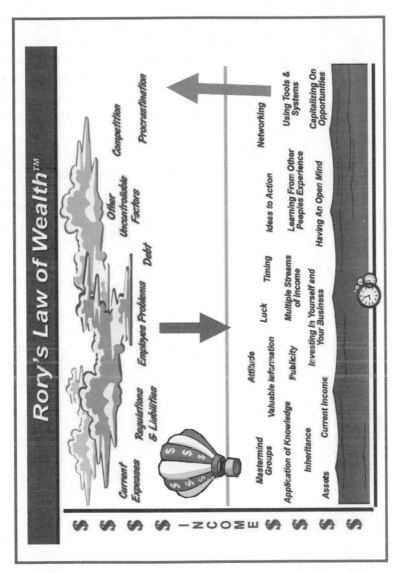

Professional Practices

From 1983 to 1987, I was a founder, partner in, and speaker for the largest integrated publishing and seminar company serving the chiropractic and dental professions in the United States and Canada. Well over 10,000 doctors went through our training programs. Today, in my private coaching groups, I have three lawyers, four dentists, and a number of other professionals. I have also worked extensively with financial planners and investment advisors.

One thing that hasn't changed since the early 1980s, and probably won't change, is these professionals' queasiness and concerns and skepticism about using advertising and marketing in an aggressive manner. They are very sensitive to what they do being perceived as "professional" by their clients and patients, peers, and the general public. Truth is, their sensitivity is almost always excessive, and they do not differentiate as they should between the reactions of patients (people who give them money) and peers, competitors, and assorted critics (people who don't give them money). I've learned that getting professionals over their own emotional blocks is as important as giving them effective marketing. You will find both Dr. Martin and Dr. Altadonna discuss this in the next two chapters.

If you are any kind of professional, in any kind of practice, these chapters are for you.

CHAPTER 11

Courageous Marketing, Marketing-Based Courage
Dr. Ben Altadonna

We've learned something in the chiropractic profession that I believe carries over to all other professional practices and many other businesses—that most businesspeople are cowards! By that I mean, they cowardly accept any and every patient, client or customer they can get, let them completely dictate the way the relationship works, and then they are often miserable because of it. Using the chiropractic practice as an example, I'd like to tell you how to change that.

**How to Double Your Practice, Increase Patient
Referrals, and Make More Money by Cutting Your
Fees and Letting Your Patients Walk All Over
Your Recommendations, Your Office Staff, and You!**

If the paradoxical headline above seems a little crazy to you, this chapter will be worth quite a bit of money to you. If you think it makes complete sense—it will be worth even more.

Here's why: I'm sure you remember the saga of the runaway bride. You know, the woman who faked her own disappearance a couple days before her wedding.

From what the news has reported, she had the audacity to terrify her fiancé and family just because she got cold feet. I can still see her father, breaking down in tears, as he pleaded for his daughter's life on the national news.

Not only did she do nothing as the police spent $60,000.00 of taxpayer's money searching for her—she allowed her fiancé to go through hell because he had become the number-one suspect.

Then, she called from Las Vegas and concocted a story that she was abducted and had escaped from her kidnappers . . . or . . . they let her go. I'm not sure which version she used.

Whatever.

Sobbing crocodile tears as she boldface lied to her devastated fiancé.

Remember that story?

Well, let me ask you a question: If YOU were the fiancé . . . and all that happened to you . . .

**Would You Stay with Her and
Go Through with the Wedding?**

I don't know what YOU would do, but, I know her fiancé has stated on the news that he plans to stay with her and marry her.

I have one word . . . WOW!

So, what does all this have to do with your practice and that nut-so headline above?

Here's what: There are several chiropractic consultants teaching EXACTLY what I stated in that headline.

- They say NOT to have high prices.
- They say NOT to mandate patients accept your full treatment plan. Let them make their own, coming and going as they choose a relief care plan.

The consultants' excuse for this "expert advice" is that high prices and making patients stick to a treatment plan *decreases* referrals.

Really?

The answer to increasing referrals and making more money is

Letting the Inmates
Run the Asylum?

Let me go back to the fiancé in the "runaway bride" story. I'm not going to judge anyone's actions . . . but . . . does the groom really think things are going to get any better? Does he really think someone who is willing to terrify her family members and let them go through what she caused—because of her unbelievably selfish act—is GOOD ENOUGH FOR HIM?

And that's what it really boils down to: WHAT YOU DECIDE AND ACCEPT AS GOOD ENOUGH FOR YOU!

Let's be honest. What kind of practice are you going to have if you accept all new patients ON THEIR TERMS?

What kind of practice are you going to have if you let new patients make their own schedules—coming and going as they please?

How much money are you going to make if you lower your price to what you THINK patients expect . . . or . . . are willing to pay?

How much is your stress, strain, and work going to INCREASE if you fill your practice with these cheapskate losers?

I bet it will do wonders for your self-esteem to let your patients walk all over you in "your" practice.

Pfui.

Cowards practice like that. Cowards practice scared. Cowards accept patients on their terms or at a discount because they NEED them. Cowards don't make any REAL money, hate their practice, and end up having nervous breakdowns. And, it's all because . . .

Cowards Don't Know
How to Market!

These consultants tell clients to practice this way because they don't know how to market effectively to get enough patients so they can practice on *their* terms.

When you master the secrets in my system and this book, you will easily generate so many patients you will have to start turning them away. When that happens, it's like magic.

You have the ability to pick and choose who you accept, how much you charge, and patients WILL stick to their treatment plan . . .

Or You Will
Drop Them from Care!

Will price be a factor like they say it is? No way. When your marketing is good enough, price is almost a nonfactor. Is there a point where your price is too high and it hurts your practice?

Absolutely. If you keep raising your prices, you will eventually hit a point of diminishing marginal return, a point where the increased price point decreases your NET.

Pay attention here—this is extremely important. It is also what these "expert consultants" don't understand.

I said "decreases your NET." Notice, I did NOT say, "decreases your total number of visits."

We are not concerned with "visits." "Visits" don't pay bills or get you that new Mercedes you've been drooling over. Visits are nothing more than work, and possibly more care than some people need.

What we are concerned with is NET. If you double your price and your visits decrease by 25%, is that bad? Not for me, partner. I'm banking a heck of a lot more money while working less.

And that is the ONLY goal of a business . . .

Maximum Profit

in Minimum Time

with the Least Work!

You may *choose* to "serve" more people or serve more people more often. You may *enjoy* seeing more visits. That's all well and good. But those are PERSONAL decisions . . . not *business* decisions.

And if you enjoy the type of people you are attracting at a discount that tell you how they are going to be treated, I'm happy for you. Don't change a thing. This is for doctors who want to practice and make money on *their* terms.

So what about referrals? Do high prices and making patients comply with their treatment plans cut down on referrals like these "experts" claim?

Let's deal with the high-price-kills-referrals garbage first.

For the high-price-kills-referral theory to be correct, all high-priced businesses would have poor referrals. Hmmm.

I guess super-high fee cosmetic surgeons don't get any referrals?

I guess no one refers to high-priced stores like Neiman Marcus or Tiffany's? All the businesses on Rodeo Drive must, somehow, find a way to operate . . . *100% Referral-Free!*

I guess Dan Kennedy, who is the highest priced copywriter I am aware of, charging as high as $70,000.00 for a sales letter campaign (yes 70 thousand!) doesn't get any referrals?

We all know that's not true. And before you run wild with the old "but chiropractic is different" nonsense, it's not. *Fundamentally—all businesses, all practices are the same.*

Before we get to some specific about all this, allow me to go on the record and say . . .

Who Cares about Referrals?

Let's say you raise your prices and make people comply. You build the practice you like to work in, and you make a ton of money. But, NO ONE REFERS!

Darn. You've got your dream practice and no one is referring. SO WHAT. Just keep marketing. It's that simple.

Why on earth would you want a referral practice when it's filled with the wrong people? Why not just continue marketing and get what you want?

And if you lower your price and accept people on their terms, your practice will be filled with patients you hate, and you will not make as much money as you could and should.

Why? Because like refers like. The patients that don't respect you will refer family and friends that walk all over you. Cheapskates will refer cheapskates. That's just the way it works. You will have a perpetual referral nightmare!

Think about this: Do you really want to establish yourself and be known as the "cheap doctor?" Think about it . . .

But here's where it gets good: If you choose *not* to be a coward, to charge high fees, and to only accept patients on your terms . . .

They Will Refer More
Just Like Themselves!

Will you get as many as all the dead-beats you got because you were cheap and let them tell you what to do? Maybe not. But you don't need as many. Remember, these new patients are worth more. So once again, you work less and make more while treating only the patients you enjoy

I'll say it again: LIKE REFERS LIKE.

If you want cheap patients that tell you how to run your practice and you hate to treat, accept them, and they will fill your practice will more just like themselves.

Almost every time I've ever heard Dan Kennedy speak, someone in the crowd has raised a hand and said something to the effect that they have a practice filled with patients that are cheap, lazy, stupid, won't listen to them, don't respect them, etc. Basically, the practice is filled with patients they hate.

Dan's response is ALWAYS the same . . .

"Who Brought them There?"

Who brought them in your practice, and who accepted them for care? And, if you don't like them, why the heck don't you change them?

I'll tell you why most don't change them. They don't know how. But, if you stick with me, you will know EXACTLY what to do.

If you do the correct marketing and only accept top-dollar, compliant patients you love—AND DO ALL THE PROPER THINGS ONCE YOU GET THEM—that's what they will refer.

I laugh when I hear these "experts" teaching doctors to be cowards because they don't know how to market and build a practice *correctly*. They are so scared, they have to bow down and accept *whatever* stumbles in the door.

Listen. There is only so much crap you can take from people whether it's in your personal life or practice.

Chiropractors have been treated like second-class citizens for a long, long time. Beat down by greedy insurance companies, ignorant medical doctors, and biased press.

Now we have "consultants" and "coaches" adding insult to injury amplifying the problem by advising you to lower your prices and let patients, who have no chiropractic training whatsoever, decide when and how often they should come.

Does this advice make any sense to you at all?

Taking the path of least resistance because you are afraid to confront your patients . . . because you don't know where the next one is coming from . . . is no way to practice. It's also no way to live your life.

A Life of Scarcity and Fear.

And . . . no matter how hard you try . . . you can't hide what's REALLY going on. How do you think society, colleagues, and even your family and friends view you if you practice this way?

Be honest with yourself. What's your impression of a struggling doctor that discounts fees, begs patients to stay, and lets them make up their own treatment plans?

And the worst thing is that this image feeds on itself and only gets worse . . . unless you takes the proper steps to change it.

- *Wouldn't it be better* to be the highest priced doctor in town?
- *Wouldn't it be better* to walk around with your head held high in your practice and community because you are respected and valued for what you do?
- *Wouldn't it be better* to be able to give your family whatever they want—whenever they want it. Never having to disappoint them (ever again) by saying no and never having to live month to month and skimp just to get by because you never have to worry about new patients or money again?
- *Wouldn't it be better* to have all that than simply cringe in the corner, accept defeat, and get by on life's meager scraps? All because you don't ACT on the information you have at your fingertips.

The bottom line is: it doesn't have to be that way. With the skills I teach, you can create *any* practice and *any* life you want. You can have the respect of your patients and community . . . make almost as much money as you want . . . give your family all the best things in life . . . while working as little or as much as you want.

Sounds like a dream . . . doesn't it?

Well, it's not. And it's not luck either.

Success like I have described above is the result of applying the right knowledge under the right circumstances. And then systematizing it so you can multiple the success and cut down on the amount of work it takes to achieve the same results. Systemization also enables you to have someone else do the work . . . so you work less.

Success is NOT determined by hard work. If you think it is, just look around. Every day I see hard workers struggling to pay their bills and get ahead. Ditch diggers work harder than you or I ever will. And, they can dig harder and harder every day without making their paychecks or lives one bit better.

Success is also NOT determined by talent. There are countless talented people starving. The same holds true for intelligence.

What really matters is finding the shortcut and applying where it is most likely to work. At that point, it's all about persistence.

But, without the shortcut . . . without the insider information . . . you will forever be like a dog chasing its tail, working harder and harder while getting further and further away from your goal.

Unless you get lucky. Which does happen from time to time. But, I wouldn't bank on luck. And while we are on the subject of luck . . .

Beware of taking advice from someone whose success was nothing more than the product of a set of lucky circumstances. Most of the time, those lucky circumstances will never be repeated.

For example, take chiropractors who built big practices during the '70s and '80s. Drop these guys and gals in a new town today to build a practice from scratch, and most would be bankrupt in less then a year.

Being lucky enough to become a chiropractor when all you had to do was put out a sign and people swarmed does not make you an expert practice builder.

The expert practice builder has the correct knowledge, strategies, and turn-key systems to build a very successful practice in just 120 days or less . . . TODAY . . . IN ANY TOWN.

Dr. Altadonna is the undisputed chiropractic new patient and practice building authority and is sought out by all types of small- and medium-sized businesses and entrepreneurs for business building strategies. Currently over 5,500 doctors of chiropractic worldwide use Ben's strategies to attract only patients who will pay, stay, and refer. To learn more about Ben, seminars, products, and services, go to www.benaltadonna.com.

CHAPTER 12

Direct Response Marketing for Dentists and Other Professionals
Dr. Charles Martin

D entists and other professionals seem more reluctant than other business owners to use effective direct response marketing. I long ago erased my reluctance, and have become a champion of this approach.

As a practicing dentist, teacher, advisor, and coach for dentists, professionals, and small business owners, I often get asked, "How can I get more new patients?" or "How can I get more *quality* new patients?"

These are *simple questions with complex answers.* The complexity disappears as you clear away the fog that surrounds 99% of every professional's practice.

If you feel unhappy with your marketing, then the first place to look isn't your marketing! Look first at the five primary questions you must answer that *enable* your marketing to work.

Here are first four primary questions to apply to your practice:

1. What do you want to accomplish? (Goals)
2. Why do you want to accomplish these things? (Purposes)
3. What makes you and your services unique, different, appealing, and preferred? (Strategy)
4. Who do you want to serve? Where do they live? Age? Income? How do they think? Interests? What are the demographics and psychographics? (Target market)

Your thoughtful, deliberate consideration of these four questions and your subsequent answers create the *foundation for your success.*

Frankly, most professionals and small business entrepreneurs have usually skipped these questions or only partially answered them.

The ugly truth: even when you do answer them once, you still have to *keep answering them* because everything around you is changing and evolving. Life continues to move ever faster, and you had better move with it or get left behind.

The big fifth question is:

5. How can you *communicate* who you are and what you do so others *want* and *prefer* your services?

Another way to say this is how can you use public relations, marketing, and sales to gain patients who say yes to your highest and best services? This is still a strategic question.

Strong strategies dominate. There are hundreds of tactics you *could* use. Most will be a waste of time and money until you answer the primary questions. My clients tell me that our work together frees them from hundreds of hours of painful guessing and uncertainty. *Your marketing strategy decides your tactics.*

Marketing Principles

There are principles to lay as a foundation for building your marketing machine. Here are seven of the most important.

> ## Resource
>
> You can get a more complete list of these kinds of Marketing Foundation Questions, from Dr. Martin and other experts, in the free e-mail course that expands this book at www.nobsbooks.com.

1. Authenticity. Being who you are is good enough. Trying to be what you aren't just tires you out. Plus, there will be plenty of people who will like you just as you prefer to be.

2. Engage the thoughts that are already going on in your potential patient's mind. Connecting with the worldview that already exists in your patient's mind makes it easier to gain agreement. If you can get the agreement with the viewpoint that your patient already has, you get someone who wants to listen to what you have to say.

3. The strength of your message is more important than how you say it. If you speak to the heart, the mind will follow.

4. Get others to say about you what you can't say. Let others brag you up. Your patients will more easily believe what other patients and your staff say about you.

Warning! Red Alert!
Your Marketing May Not Be
Your Biggest Problem!

For a dentist, or any professional, the goal of your marketing is to get your phone to ring. *Marketing done well* does the majority of your selling for you. It *pre-persuades* your prospective patient/client to say yes to you *before* you offer services.

How well the phone is handled is either a gi-normous problem or equally gi-normous opportunity. (Gi-normous is defined as giant and enormous according to my four daughters, age 15 to 25.) I have discovered a disease of epidemic proportions in the mishandling of the phone. Sadly, 95% of all offices have this disease in some form. This problem is responsible for the waste of thousands of dollars of marketing money and tens of thousands of lost income monthly.

I agree with you: it sounds unbelievable. *The truth is still true no matter how much you and I would like it to be different.* If you are concerned about the total impact on your practice, I suggest you take a look at the complete description of the problem and the opportunity of my total solution on my web site at www.AffluentPracticeSystems.com.

5. Measure. Keep statistics on what marketing is working. If a marketing tactic isn't working, stop it. If it is working, discover ways to do more. The key here is to monitor objectively using numbers.

6. The power of your attraction is directly proportional to the strength of your repulsion. Consider the Howard Stern effect. You either like him or don't like him. There are very few middle-of-the-road viewpoints when you consider him. Who you want to attract will be enhanced by who you want to repel. This one is tough for most of us in health care. If you try to be everything to everybody, you aren't anything to anyone!

7. Know the math. How much you can spend on marketing is directly proportional to the value of your average patient over the period of time he/she is your patient. This is called the *lifetime value*. It is leveraged by how many referrals you get on average from each patient multiplied by their LPV (lifetime patient value.)

Dissecting an Actual Direct Response Ad

Once you have a solid marketing foundation, then—and only then—can you begin developing and using really effective direct response ads, web sites and other marketing media. With that said, let's look at an actual direct response ad, Figure 12.2, which appears at the end of this chapter.

Direct response can be used well in many media, including newspaper, television, radio, Yellow Pages, direct mail, web sites, speeches, and even public relations.

The hallmark of a direct response ad is *the call to action*—to *act now* as a result of the ad.

As a professional, your marketing should reflect who you are and what you do and why patients should choose you.

A Common Mistake Most Professionals Make

The ad is *about* the professional provider! No! No! No! This is hugely popular with ad makers as they know it is easy to get a yes from the doctor for the proposed ad.

Your prospective patient has the viewpoint that the ad should be about them. It is as if each one says, "Is it about me, my wants and needs, that's what I care about!" Headlines that reflect this viewpoint are successful. All others are hit and miss. *Your ad and headline should be all about the prospective patient and the benefits he/she can get by using your services.* Your ad isn't about you. It is about them.

Let Testimonials Say What You Can't

In today's culture, the direct message gets resisted. If you make a claim directly, you had better back it up very strongly. Skepticism is rampant. People have been fooled so many times by government and big corporations like Enron, WorldCom, and Tyco that the first response to any message made directly is disbelief. The direct message of quality has been claimed so many times that it's a waste of time.

You can still promote quality or any other concept indirectly *using what others say about you.* What others say about you is 1,000 times more believable than what you say. Moreover, patients will say good things about you that you would be too embarrassed to say yourself!

"Tell Me a Story"

Our culture loves a good story. Stories are how we are taught as young children. As adults, we love a good story. What the Bible and Ronald Reagan (the great communicator) have in common are the use of stories to spread a message. Oprah Winfrey has created a billion dollar empire from the human interest *stories* she helps spin and weave into the fabric of her daily television show.

Testimonials are stories—the success stories of your patients/clients. They get through the incessant barrage of marketing messages *to deliver your message like no other*. They can and should be used in every media you can think of (even the walls of your offices).

Stories in testimonial form are powerful, emotion-evoking carriers for your message. Your patient's testimonial creates a natural identification with your potential patient. "That's me" is the natural response after reading it. They put themselves into the story. That is exactly where you want them, seeing a positive, well-formed outcome in the future as the result of working with you.

Testimonials Benefit from Good Headlines

Headlines are there to grab attention and compel interest in reading more. They are the "ad for the ad." You can see the difference between a good headline and a weak one. A good one is like a magnet, it pulls you to it. You can even hear it—it's the sound of the phone ringing—the sound of 2 calls *vs.* 20 calls.

Use a Picture of Your Patient

Pictures draw the eye to them. They give a visual impact that works alone *and* to support the patient's story. Choose a picture that reflects and resonates with your target market. If possible, include age and occupation. These help create further identification and agreement with your potential patient. This is all part of *making your message match your market.*

The Body Copy

The copy itself should do two things. First, it agrees with what a prospective patient thinks about your services. This has been called "the world view" by Seth Godin. Robert Collier calls this agreeing "with the conversation already going on in the person's mind." *The more agreement you create, the better able you are to convey your message.*

Second, the copy should impart information and benefits about using your services. *The strength of your message is more important than the strength of your copy.* A weak message said well will still perform weakly. A strong message said well can yield explosive results.

The Strength of Your Offer Influences Response

The hallmark of direct response is the offer to stimulate the reader/listener/viewer to do something *now*. The stronger the offer, the more response you will get.

Your direct response ad does not need to give away profits to work. You should calculate your average new patient lifetime value so you know how valuable each new patient is for you.

Then you can make a common sense decision on how much you can afford to offer to get a new patient (and maintain an existing one). Along with the offer, it would be smart to give an argument compelling enough to stand alone, to give reasons why your prospective patient should become your patient.

The offer in the ad in Figure 12.1 is for a free initial consultation. This is considered professional enough to be acceptable. I suggest bumping your offer based on your need for new patients. I don't need many, so this offer fits for me.

Give Multiple Ways to Respond

In this ad, you'll notice three ways to respond. The one we want—*call us*—is promoted first.

The second way to answer is by requesting more information via an 800 toll-free number. This gives the interested but uncertain prospect a risk-free way to get more information and allows us to continue the marketing process. This method allows us to gather information so we can continue to market to these potential new patients in multiple steps. This is traditional *lead generation marketing*.

The third way, the web site, is least preferred, but as web sites are now standard for any professional, it continues the process. Web sites should be designed with more testimonials and information because some people need more of both before deciding to act. Lead generation can start from a web site as well.

Charles W. Martin, DDS, MAGD, DICOI, FIADFE, is in private practice in Richmond, Virginia, providing holistic cosmetic dentistry, longevity dentistry, and "Martin Method Dentistry" to patients who come to his unique office from all over the world. He is the founder of Affluent Practice Systems and provides high-level coaching to dentists throughout the United States and Canada. For information, go to www.AffluentPracticeSystems.com or call (866) 263-5577.

FIGURE 12.1: Dr. Charles Martin's Direct Response Advertisement

New Permanent Teeth Help Local Virginian Find Relief

By: Ron Ellis

"Not many of us take care of our teeth like we should. We let some things go unattended like I did. I was not diligent in going to the dentist or the hygienist like I should have.

Everyone should realize when you age (even though there are a few people who will have great teeth for a hundred years) and you reach your fifties to mid fifties your teeth are going to show stains, chips, and just plain wear out. A great way to gain confidence and feel good about yourself is to have your teeth redone. It is a wonderful thing to have a nice smile!

I have had extensive dental treatment done by Dr. Charles Martin, including implants. On a scale of 1 to 10, I would rate his office a 10 plus! Dr. Martin wants you to feel comfortable all the time. All of my treatment was very successful and at no time did I feel any pain.

My mouth looks excellent and my experience in this office was exceptional. Dr. Martin's work is the best and I would never consider changing to another dentist.

I recommend this dental practice to everyone. I am very, very satisfied with my dental care. Check our this smile!!"

To schedule an examination call today. Dr. Martin will be pleased to evaluate you and answer your questions regarding implants. Uncertain? Call our Dental Information Hotline at 800-303-3064 ext. 2747 and request your FREE Special Report: How To Get The Smile You Want With Dental Implants.

The dentist recommended by other dentists
"With his caring touch and advanced training in Implant Dentistry, Dr. Charles Martin in Richmond stands out. He has helped so many people who thought there was no way to save their teeth achieve beautiful smiles! Dr. Martin is a leader in the dental field, no question about it!"

Dr. Brian Hirschfeld, D.D.S.
Livonia, NY

Dr. Charles Martin, D.D.S., & Associates

Where you get the smile you want

11201 Huguenot Road
Richmond, VA
www.MartinSmiles.com
(804) 320-6800
or call toll free
(866) 263-5577

to schedule your *Free* initial Consultation
Or call our Dental Information Hotline at
(800) 303-3064 ext. 2747
to request your FREE Special Report about
The Miracle of Dental Implants.

Actual Implant Patient of Dr. Charles Martin.

Sales Careers

For more than 25 years, I have been talking to sales professionals about replacing old-fashioned, unpleasant manual labor prospecting, especially "cold" prospecting, with far more effective direct marketing. This idea is very important for sales professionals, sales managers, and business owners employing salespeople. Here's why: if you are a hospital administrator with a highly trained, celebrated, expert heart surgeon on staff, you surely do not want that surgeon also mopping the floors or talking on the phone to prospective patients who haven't first been screened as to appropriateness for care, ability to pay, etc. No! You want that surgeon doing surgery. If you are the surgeon and the hospital administrator hands you a mop, you should use it to beat him to a bloody pulp. Similarly, a good sales pro should spend his time selling.

Scott Tucker's chapter that follows piggybacks on this idea and should provide great inspiration to any sales professional.

A lot of salespeople, as well as business owners, incorrectly view making a sale as an incident and an outcome, something that is done when the customer signs on the dotted line. But the most successful sales professionals I know and work with think differently. They view it as just one part of a process. Al Williams' chapter addresses this brilliantly.

If you are in any sales field, you can profit enormously by following up on the ideas introduced in these chapters. If you own a business employing salespeople or manage salespeople, these chapters should encourage you to change the way you support your salespeople and give you ideas for better working with your salespeople to increase their productivity.

CHAPTER 13

How to Keep Clients Informed, Interested, Happy, and Coming Back for More
Al Williams

I operate in a business where there is an extended period between the time my sales process begins and ends. I'm a commercial lender, working with investors buying apartment buildings and commercial properties, but many others have similar circumstances, including real estate brokers, insurance agents waiting for policy underwriting after the sale, even lawyers. There are other analogus businesses. My objective is to over-communicate with my clients so they have no anxiety, so they feel appreciated, so they will want to business with me again.

For that purpose, I developed what I call Pacific Northwest Capital's Seven-Step Customer Care System. You may or may not want to use mine as a model, but you should definitely have some *system* of your own.

So, let's look at my business as an example.

Almost all investors who have ground through the commercial loan process will tell you it isn't fun. The typical approval process usually takes six weeks or more, and extreme patience, because lenders continuously seem to ask for more and more documentation. It can be frustrating, contentious, and downright boring.

In spite of all of the obstacles that lenders place in the path of an investor, the number one complaint investors have about the loan process is the lack of communication between themselves and the lender/broker once their loan application has been submitted. Few lenders or brokers take the time or make the effort during the loan process to keep the investor informed and up-to-date with the progress of their loan file.

Our position is that each and every investor who has a loan application pending with our company, along with all real estate brokers and anyone else involved in a transaction, must be "touched" by our company at least once each week, from the moment they apply for financing with us right up through the closing of their transactions.

The easiest and most efficient weekly touch is our Friday fax/e-mail Status Report. This is just a very simple fax or e-mail message sent each Friday to our investors and involved agents outlining the progress we made on their loan application during the past week and setting expectations for the week ahead. Not much new or different with this concept, but very few lenders or brokers even invest this much effort in a client.

However, in order to truly separate our company from the hordes of other commercial brokerage firms, we take our client contact system a huge step further. We have added a Seven-Step contact system to the process, with each contact or mailing built around a significant threshold or milestone reached in the loan process itself. Included in this system are items or "gifts" that are mailed periodically to the investor that are somewhat relevant to the point where we are in the processing of his loan application. The gifts we send with each mailing are intended to be not only rewards for choosing us as their financing representative but to also send items that are practical for his personal use. In addition, all gifts sent are either screened or laser engraved with our company logo, address, and contact numbers. This gives us the opportunity to have several different items in the investor's home or business that display our company information. The following is an outline of each step and a capsule summary of the letter that goes with the gift.

Step 1.
The Flashlight Letter

Once you got them committed to working with you, congratulate them for making that choice!

Within a day or two after submitting their loan applications and agreeing to let our company handle the financing of their income properties, the investors (and all real estate agents involved in the transaction if this is a purchase) receive via Priority Mail a Mag-Lite flashlight in a gift box along with a "congratulatory" letter. The flashlight is in our company color (royal blue), and it has our company name and 800 number laser engraved on the barrel.

The letter is personalized and begins with the headline:

CONGRATULATIONS!
You've seen the Light!

We congratulate the investor for choosing our firm, calling it a very "enlightened" decision. We reinforce the investor's decision by acknowledging that we are being trusted with the very important task of getting his loan request approved and funded. We remind him, however, that we are the best in the business and that savvy real estate investors have trusted us with their most important commercial real estate financing needs for over 20 years.

It is our first step in establishing expectations with the investor and any real estate agents involved. We outline exactly what the investor and agents can expect from us in terms of efficiency and communication. It also introduces everyone involved to the people in our office who will be working on their files and encourages them to call us anytime with questions or concerns.

The letter ends with another big "thank you" for choosing us and a statement that the flashlight should come in handy as well as serve as a reminder that they "saw the light" in choosing our firm.

This initial contact with both the borrower and agents involved invariably breeds all kinds of positive comments and goodwill. The gift is totally unexpected and serves as an initial indication of how working with our firm is going to be different than any commercial income property financing experience they might have had. It also puts something useful in their hands that just happens to have our name and phone number on it!

Step 2.
The Clock Letter

A very important part of the loan process early on is getting the borrower to provide us with the information we need to process the loan request in a timely fashion.

This again is sent Priority Mail to the borrower (with one sent to each real estate broker involved as well) that contains a round analog desk clock with our company name and phone number strategically engraved on the base of the clock, a constant reminder of who the gift came from. We also enclose a $5.00 gift card for Starbucks and a personalized letter. The letter thanks the borrower for choosing us, or in the case of a broker, thanks him for referring the borrower to us. It also acknowledges that our senior loan processor has already contacted him with a list of items (the Needs List) that we will need in order to complete his file for underwriting.

We send the CLOCK to acknowledge the importance of *Time* in the transaction, both their time and ours, in essence urging them to respond to our questions or request for documentation just as quickly as humanly possible.

The headline at the end of the letter reads,

Sit back, relax, and have a latte on us!

The letter ends by suggesting that they should find our loan process efficient and relatively painless. However, if at any time they feel "stressed out" by the whole process, they can use the enclosed Starbucks card and enjoy a nice soothing latte on us. Once again, an unexpected gift has arrived with our name and phone number on it.

Step 3.
The "StressChek Ruler" Letter

The next milestone in the loan process is the point at which the loan file gets shipped to the underwriting department.

By the third or fourth week into the process, our office is usually ready to ship the completely processed loan file to underwriting. The day the file leaves our office, we mail out another gift and another Starbucks card along with a letter marking this milestone in the process. Again, everyone connected to the transaction receives this mailing.

The letter informs the investor that his file has been sent to underwriting and that we are now waiting for the underwriting process to take place (depending on the lender, this could take from three days to several weeks). The large headline right below the opening paragraph reads:

Warning—Waiting for Formal Loan Approval
May Be Stressful!

We send them our popular "StressChek Ruler." This is a hard white plastic ruler with a fun-to-use "press sensor" on the front, which measures heat and moisture from a person's finger or thumb. This measurement is converted to a color which equates to a level of stress (or in some cases, the level of calmness). We encourage the borrower to test his stress level at this point with the ruler.

The next heading then goes on to say:

Stress Relief Enclosed!

This encourages the client to use the enclosed Starbucks card and enjoy another latte on us. The letter ends by acknowledging that the loan should be approved soon and says to call our office with any questions they may have.

Step 4.
The Portfolio Pouch Letter

Perhaps the most important and most enjoyable part of the loan process is notifying the investor that his loan has been approved.

Immediately upon loan approval, we send the investor another gift with a letter. The letter congratulates him on the approval of his loan and the gift is a very useful Portfolio Pouch. This is an oversized plastic or leather pouch with our company information and logo and is used to store legal documents. The accompanying letter encourages the borrower to use this pouch to store the onslaught of paper that will be coming their way as they move through the loan closing process.

Step 5.
The Personalized Thank-You Card

Thanking everyone involved in the transaction immediately upon the closing of the loan is extremely important.

A day after the loan closes, we send out a very unique thank-you card to the borrower and the agents involved in the transaction. Our card was specially designed for us by a local greeting card company and features drawings of apartment or office buildings on the front. A very personalized message on the inside again thanks those involved for trusting us with the transaction and goes on to mention that they will be receiving another gift in the mail from us shortly.

Step 6.
The Gift Basket

Everyone likes to receive food in the mail!

Within the week after loan closing, we send the borrower and real estate brokers each a very nice basket of fruit, cheeses, wines, or a combination of all three. The baskets come with a small card again thanking them for their business.

Step 7.
The Testimonial Request Letter

As important as any other step, asking for a testimonial at the end of the process is crucial.

We have developed a letter that goes out to borrowers and agents at the end of the process encouraging them to write a testimonial letter on our behalf. We make sure that they receive our request within two or three days AFTER they have received their gift baskets in the mail. The theory here is that they should be feeling, if nothing else, somewhat guilty about all of the gifts and attention they have received from us during the loan process and should be more than willing at this point to write down a few kinds words about our company and our staff.

To make it as easy as possible for them to respond, we outline the type

Resource

A copy of the kind of testimonial form mentioned by Al and a copy of a testimonial advertisement are both included in the free e-mail course that expands on this book, available at www.nobsbooks.com.

of questions that we would like them to address in their letters AND provide them with stamped and addressed envelopes in which to mail the letter back to us.

Also included in the letter is another Starbucks coffee card (yes, we do own stock in Starbucks)! We point out that the coffee card is a token of our appreciation for them taking the time to forward their comments to us and also suggest that the card is theirs to use regardless of whether they respond to our request.

We have found that about 50% of investors and real estate brokers actually do sit down and write a testimonial letter for us. Since we close over 200 commercial loans each year, that gives us well in excess of 100 new testimonial letters annually that we can use as part of our marketing efforts.

Will a System Like this Work for You?

Perhaps you are thinking that this is just too much. How could you ever afford to implement a system like this, and where would you get the time to develop and implement it? Our position is that we cannot afford NOT to use this system as a way of separating us from virtually all other lenders and mortgage brokers in our market areas.

Is the dollar cost of the system worth it?

If you add up the cost of all the gifts that we send, including the coffee cards and the cost of Priority Mail postage and paper, we end up spending about *$125.00 total* on each investor and real estate agent. If our average collected fee per transaction is in *excess of $15,000.00*, you be the judge as to whether we can afford to use this system.

Al Williams is president of Pacific Northwest Capital, a leading commercial lending organization primarily working with California and Pacific Northwest investors. He is also a speaker, trainer, and consultant to both lenders and investors. For more information, visit www.apartmentfinancing.com or call (800) 265-3860.

CHAPTER 14

How Direct Marketing Can Change
Your Entire Business Life
Scott Tucker

D an Kennedy often tells us that we shouldn't limit ourselves by thinking only about how much money we can make but to also think about how we make the money. That means what kind of clients we have, how we get them, whether we go to them or they come to us, how respectful and pleasant they are to deal with, and whether they haggle over price or not. I'm a mortgage broker, and I work in an industry where most people work very hard for their money. I don't.

Learning how to use direct marketing has changed my entire life. Maybe my story will motivate you to use it to change yours!

Many mortgage brokers and loan officers do little if any *real* marketing at all. While this is a business where you can make a great deal of money, the vast majority suffer instead.

Why is this the case?

Simply because most brokers and loan officers (l.o.'s) don't know squat about *direct response* marketing. When you ask them how they measure return on investment (ROI) on whatever marketing dollars they do spend, you get blank stares. And then "What do you mean?"

Most in my business still rely on "cold" prospecting by phone or in person. Many run rate/price ads, then talk to dozens to hundreds of people, fighting every step of the way to get an appointment, then make a sale. Their ignorance, I think stubborn ignorance, of direct marketing, their sticking to all this hard work, is very good news for me and the small number of mortgage brokers I coach!

I Got Fired and I Became a Direct Marketer

I went from 0 to 60 very quickly when I first ventured out on my own, having been fired by a broker I used to work for. I turned lemons into lemonade.

How did I do it? I paid BIG bucks to shortcut the learning curve. I paid the most when I had the least. I depended upon credit cards back then to get me the *information* I needed to prosper in the following months.

Most, men especially, are too stubborn to admit that there might be *something,* maybe just one thing, they don't know. I just knew that I had to "check and see" if maybe there was something I didn't know, something that would make my way to the top easier, quicker, and "cheaper" overall. Cheaper when considering all the waste I would commit if I was in the dark in any way.

I wasn't sure how I wanted to or could change the mortgage business, but I was determined to find or invent a better way than I had experienced while working for the other broker.

I remember the first thing I bought was Dan's newsletter. Back then it was only something like $200.00 a year for the Silver Membership. I thought that was a big deal: "Geez, 200 bucks? Okay, I guess I'll try 'er out."

After the first issue, I was hooked. What I found was a lot different from everything I'd been taught and had been doing. Somehow, I just knew this new information was gonna make me a fortune. I saw examples of how it was doing just that for others in other businesses. I knew that if direct response marketing could work for pest control, carpet cleaners, house painters, and all of that, that it would work even better if there was a higher ticket thing to sell, such as a mortgage.

I went on to spend $100.00 here, $500.00 there, and so on, on just about every direct response audio course I could find. I studied at the feet of the direct response masters—people like Dan Kennedy, Jeff Paul, John Carlton, Gary Halbert, Ted Nicholas, and the list goes on and on.

I bought every direct response book ever written, or so it seemed. Victor Schwab, Denny Hatch, Joe Karbo, Joe Sugarman, all of them. I've got a storage room and several bookcases full of books, tapes, CDs, etc.

I devoured all this information. Morning, noon, and night. Weekends. Whatever it took. When I was younger, I'd spent five years active duty in the Navy, so this wasn't really any "hard work" in my opinion. Even though all my friends were amazed at how "hard" I was working on getting up to speed in direct response, I told them that I used to work 100-hour weeks at sea in the Navy for $13,000.00 a year, sometimes supervising up to 40 people. So this was a much better deal!

The First Mailing

My first mailing cost me about $5,000.00. I knew it would work, but then again I wasn't real sure either. Know what I mean? The $5,000.00 was the most I'd ever spent on something you drop in a mailbox! I hoped like heck the phone would ring.

The very next day, that phone was ringing nonstop. It was then that I wondered if I really should have dropped all 5,000 letters all at once! But what was done was done, so there was nothing I could do but just take and return all the calls as best I could.

The sales letter I had written took me about three months to write, so it had to work. Had to be perfect. So-so wouldn't cut it. I was at the plate, but only allowed one pitch. It had to get hit out of the park, or I'd have to go back to working for a broker where leads are provided but the commission split would be lousy. I'd just about rather work for the government than do that again.

The phone rang from early morning until late at night. At night, after about 10:00 P.M. or so, I'd unplug the phone and let it go to voicemail. I thought it might seem kinda weird to folks if I was still answering the phone at 3:00 A.M.! Plus, I was exhausted.

The only reason I took calls live from 8:00 A.M. until 10:00 P.M. was that I knew that calls answered live by me would convert to closed loans the best.

I remember the first loan I closed off of that batch. The guy closed about three to four weeks from when he first called. It was a $12,000.00 fee to me. I only do sub-prime refi's, so I'd earned my money getting him straightened out.

I was working then on an independent contractor arrangement with a broker, and that broker would pay me on a 1099. The only thing they got from it was $500.00 a file. A $12,000.00 fee, $500.00 to the broker, and $11,500.00 to yours truly. Just that one deal justified the $5,000.00 I'd spent on the mailing! Plus, there was still $6,500.00 "left over" for me to live on! I knew that if I closed no other deals off of that mailing that I'd already done good.

But that first $5,000.00 mailing returned $75,000.00 to me in about the first 60 days! I had never made that much money before. I kept on like that for about four months. Working seven days a week, mailing the same letter, to darn near the same list, until I finally needed to take some time off. I had socked away a ton in the bank, paid off my truck, and took a ten-day vacation to Europe.

Now, I kind of snicker at those numbers. Just 2 months before writing this chapter, I closed $105,300.00 in fees! I only worked 40 hours to do it. Just me, and one processor. Oh, except one Saturday that month I worked 1 hour to do a closing for someone that could close no other time.

Doing Business on My Terms

Once I saw how many good prospects I could get to call me with this kind of marketing, I started thinking a lot about how I could leverage this, to do business on my terms. As Dan says, to pay attention to making money in a way I really like.

The power of direct response marketing is amazing. I have, for a couple of years now, done 100% of my business from my office. I never meet with anyone at their office or home. My office is a commercial condo at the foot of the same building where my penthouse luxury condo is located. I have an elevator commute. My dog Boomer has an Orvis bed in my office, and he likes it that way.

Thanks to my marketing, I effortlessly have folks driving to me for the signing of the application. And I make then drive to me again for the closing. This is the only face-to-face selling I ever do. And really, the direct response marketing has done all the real selling for me, without me having exerted any effort at all.

I recently helped a couple that live over 90 minutes away from my office. Three hours round trip, *twice*. Six hours in the car, all just so "the guru" could do their loan for them. Sure, their loan was difficult, but there's someone else that could have gotten it done for them. They chose me instead, and did business 100% on my terms and to suit my desired lifestyle.

When you apply these proven direct response techniques to a business like the mortgage business, a place where no one else is using any real imagination at all, your results will be many times that of your "competitors!" In fact, there will be no competition at all!

When you talk to your prospect like you're one guy and so are they, and get all that "institutional voice" stuff out of the way, they will deal

> ### Resource
>
> To see a sample of Scott's actual advertising, and for a longer discussion of his Expert Positioning, enroll in the free e-mail course that expands on this book at www.nobsbooks.com.

with you in a way that shows a strong *personal* connection and relationship.

How to Sell with No Price Resistance

One of the things I decided about how I wanted to make money was that I did not want to deal with customers who would arm-wrestle me over my fees or the interest rates for their mortgages. That decision controls my marketing. Everything I do, from my ads and web sites to the free report/sales letter that I send prospects who respond to my ads, is written to drive off any "price wrestlers."

In my office, there is seldom any price resistance from anyone. If and when there is *any* objection to price—you know that after your whole "value presentation" has been made via your automated direct response marketing mechanisms—you know you have encountered possibly the *cheapest, least appreciative, and biggest pain-in-the-butt prospect on Earth!*

My advice? Throw them out. Refer them to a bargain basement competitor. If they want "the cheapest price," let them have it. But not in your office. You've got lives to change. If they take up your time, that's time you can't spend helping another deserving, appreciative, respectful, full-fare paying family.

In my business, I have the ability to give everyday hard-working homeowners an experience like they've never had anywhere else. To put the spotlight on *them* To treat *them* like the stars. To *change their lives.* For them to *finally* feel like someone is actually *listening,* concerned with the quality of *their* outcomes.

If you feel the way I do about the products or services you sell, or change what you sell, or who you specialize in selling to so you can feel like I do, you'll have the confidence to drive away people mostly concerned with price. You will attract better customers. Your work will be a lot more fun!

Doing It Myself

Everything I've just told you to do, I've done for myself. And I continue to do it every day. I use direct mail, voice broadcast, 24-hour free recorded messages, display ads, you name it. I use anything and everything I can get to work at a positive ROI.

Four Keys to Using Direct Marketing not Just to Make Money but to Change Your Life

1. Decide how you want to conduct business.

2. Employ direct response advertising and marketing to target and attract customers who are compatible with you and the way you want to do business.

3. Use marketing messages that position you as an expert, as the only person on earth who does exactly what you do specifically for the kind of people you want as customers.

4. Use your lead generation advertising, recorded messages, web sites, and materials you send out to repel cheapskates and other customers you don't want and to qualify prospects you do want.

I've gotten as much as 52 times ad cost on display ads in tiny niche publications and fifteen times cost on direct mail to cold, compiled lists! You name it, I've done it in this business, using direct response marketing.

I never call on a Realtor® for a deal. I never ask family and friends to send me business or referrals. Instead, I tell them I don't want them! I don't buy internet leads. I don't buy telemarketed leads either.

No one else is my source of leads. I am my own source, and I wouldn't have it any other way.

My direct response methods work so well that I literally get leads in my sleep. I'm writing this on a Saturday morning at the coffee shop. Just before starting, I opened up my e-mail and found that I had received an online application from my web site. How perfect is that?

All this is possible for you, too. It just depends upon you to make the decision to change your life.

Scott Tucker is a mortgage broker and loan offer. He is available, on a very limited basis, for consulting in a number of fields, mortgage brokerage chief among them. Mr. Tucker also operates a seminar, coaching, and consulting business for mortgage brokers and loan officers. He accepts communications from interested parties via fax and FedEx only. (No phone calls or e-mails will be accepted, nor answered. Postal mail is not recommended.) Scott Tucker, Tucker Marketing Systems, Inc., 2154 W. Roscoe St., Chicago, Illinois 60618, fax: (773) 327-2842, web site: www.mortgagemarketinggenius.com.

Service Businesses

It would be hard to find anyone, in any kind of service business, who can hold a candle to Chet Rowland's success at thoroughly and completely "systemizing" both the marketing and the operations sides of such a business.

In my Renegade Millionaire System (www.renegademillionaire.com), I teach that there's an achievement far greater than effective delegation, that the ultimate entrepreneurial accomplishment is "replacement." I apply that a number of ways. One, with regard to marketing and sales, is the replacement of manual labor prospecting or selling with automated marketing and marketing tools that work for you and produce better quality customers. As you'll see in this chapter, Chet has accomplished that. Another is to literally replace yourself with systems, so you are liberated from day-to-day operations and worries and from uncertainty about sales and revenues. You can use this liberation for pleasure or to expand your horizons, pursuing other opportunities and multiple streams of income. Chet has done this as well.

There are, in this chapter, some specific ideas and examples that can improve any service business' marketing. But there's a bigger, more important insight, too—an example of how a service business owner can enjoy a much better, more exciting business life.

CHAPTER 15

From Dead-Broke Bug Guy to
Marketing Millionaire
Chet Rowland

A story with a happy ending! In 1985, I had massive problems in my pest control business in Orlando and Tampa, Florida, and briefly considered just throwing in the towel.

I grew up in a home with no indoor plumbing or electricity. I got my first job in pest control because I was a big, strong guy who could follow directions. I did my time crawling through attics and underneath porches killing bugs. I've also employed as many as 32 people—and questioned my sanity and their stupidity daily! Through long hours, hard work, determination, and salesmanship, I went from an ordinary bug guy to the owner of a thriving business. I started from scratch and went for a long period barely surviving week to week, job to job before finally getting my business to a level of financial success. But still, it was a business that seemed to require my day-to-day, minute-by-minute personal attention, juggling selling, delivering services, managing people, and solving problems. In 1985, I was also victimized by massive embezzling in my Orlando operation, had to retreat to just the Tampa business, and, in many ways, felt I was starting over. But by far the most tiring, fatiguing, frustrating thing to me was the constant uncertainty and worry over where the next customer was coming from.

If I was going to stay in the pest control business, I was determined to do two things: figure out a different way to get and keep customers and make the business run with systems so I could make a million dollars a year and only come to the office one day a week.

It took me 20 years of struggle to get my business to the million dollar a year mark. It took only 36 months more to jump it to two million! Last year, it grew by another half-million—not by buying routes or companies, but by acquiring customers with *direct* marketing. In 1997, I discovered Dan Kennedy's *No B.S. Marketing Letter*, and that led me to his and others' direct marketing strategies nobody in pest control was using. Things began changing rapidly.

Let me fast forward. Today, my pest control company is in the top 1% of the entire industry. I live in a sprawling lakeside home, and I own several beachfront condos valued at over $4 million. I have my pest control business running so smoothly by systems that I go to the office only once or twice a month. The business is fed by a collection of what Dan calls "direct marketing systems" that provide a very stable, continuous, predictable flow of good business. I've even virtually ended employee turnover. Freed from the day-to-day slavery to that business—now a master of it—I've been able to turn my attention to real estate investing and other businesses, including providing all my advertising, marketing and business systems, and coaching to pest control operators all over the United States, Canada, and several other countries. I've made more progress, created more growth, and made more money in the past 3 years than in the previous 20 years combined! And I've worked less and had fewer headaches. That's the power of direct marketing!

Now, let me share just a few specific pieces or components of the direct marketing that fuel my pest control business and have nearly universal application to all businesses.

First, a lot of the new customers as well as the high-dollar tent fumigation jobs (to eradicate termites) are sold by lengthy sales letters—not by telemarketers, salespeople, or pest control technicians forced to be bad salespeople. When people call from our ads or, often, are referred by customers because of our referral marketing system, we send them our highly effective sales letters. The letters do all the heavy lifting When the customers call to schedule service, they are pre-sold, and they are willing to pay above average, premium prices for our services. In fact, my marketing system eliminates price competition. I spent a lot of money getting these sales letters right. When I learned about direct marketing and began trying to use it, after about six months I sensed that a big missing ingredient in my marketing was really effective sales copy. I did what no other small service business owner would do: I hired top, celebrated, very expensive direct response copywriters who typically work for big, national companies to write my sales copy. Not just one either, a number of them. I experimented, tested different sales copy, and gradually arrived at what works.

Second, one key to my marketing, my sales copy, and my competitive edge is my use of super strong guarantees. In the examples at the end of this chapter, you'll find five pages from my sales letters (Figures 15.1 through 15.5). These pages are not in order, so don't be confused. I picked pages that illustrate my daring guarantees and the way I present them. As you'll see, my guarantees are a big part of my marketing. Dan calls this "gutsy marketing," and I've found he's right about two things: most business owners don't have the guts to boldly guarantee what they sell, and two, doing so is very profitable. The fear of being burnt is not justified, providing you do good work. Only a few times all year do I have to actually pay off on a guarantee to a customer we can't satisfy, and that's a small cost compared to the selling power gained from the guarantees. And I even show prospects the letters from those customers and the refund checks—I put two at the end of this chapter (Figures 15.6 and 15.7)—so I get selling power from them, too!

Of course, these are only two peeks at a much more complete marketing system, but I hope these give you a good idea of what can be done to revolutionize a business with this kind of marketing.

The best payoff for me is the freedom. Now I have a great income from a smoothly running business and lots of free time to pursue other interests and opportunities. My business helping pest control operators, www.PCOMillionaire.com, is growing by leaps and bounds, thanks to the same kind of direct marketing. After being a lifelong bachelor for 51 years, I've even taken all my knowledge about how to meet and date exciting women and put it into books and courses, sold at www.Chet'sDating

System.com. One thing's for sure, my days as an overworked, underpaid bug guy are l-o-n-g gone!

Chet Rowland is the owner and president of Chet's Pest Control in Tampa, Florida, and of PCO Millionaire LLC, providing marketing and business systems, coaching, and consulting to pest control operators worldwide. You can contact Chet directly by fax at (813) 926-0657, e-mail chetrowland@aol.com, or visit www. pcomillionaire.com.

FIGURE 15.1: Chet Rowland's Sales Letter

Finally, The Only 100% Risk Free Money Back Guarantee In The Termite Industry… Is Here!

With my "termite tight" guarantee….

"At Last, <u>Never</u> Pay For Termite Treatments Again"

"I'm the owner of Chet's Pest Control, the company with the only checklist of 57 termite inspection points. *(One that took me 35 years to perfect.)* I'm also the owner of the only Florida bug company with a powerful renewable <u>lifetime</u> guarantee. (Believe me, if termites could read it, they'd hightail it fast and never even think of coming back.) Even better, when you call to schedule the treatment, I'll give you $225.00 in FREE bonuses!"

Both of us know, one inspection or termite treatment won't give you an gnat's head of what you really want: a termite-free home *for the rest of your life.* (Remember, <u>Florida has the highest termite infestation in the U.S.)</u> That's why I'm offering you a powerful, termite tight guarantee….

A RENEWABLE, TRANSFERRABLE THREE-PHASE GUARANTEE that lasts not just for one year, not even five, but for….a *lifetime:*

1. If, within *one* year of your first treatment, we uncover a new colony of live subterranean termites, I will re-treat your home for FREE—*and* refund your initial investment.
2. If, during the first *five* years of your service contract, we uncover a new colony of live subterranean termites, we will re-treat for FREE.
3. If, during the first five years and *any* year thereafter, we uncover a new colony of live subterranean termites, we will re-treat for FREE—EVEN IF YOU SELL THE HOME AND MOVE OUT! How can I afford such a huge long-term risk? Read on….

Dear Friend,

Face it. Not all pest control companies give termites and bugs an equally bad time. I'm sorry to say, the industry has problems: con-artists, disreputable dealers, and even national companies who cheat on their customers *(see page 3).* Shame on them! In the meantime, ten of thousands of destructive termites have been left undetected to party round the clock in hundreds of Florida homes….

Homes like yours. Without my unique 57-POINT TERMITE & PEST CONTROL

©2004 Proven Marketing Works

FIGURE 15.2: Chet Rowland's Sales Letter

Face it. Not all termite & pest control companies give termites and bugs an equally bad time. I'm sorry to say, the industry has problems: con-artists, disreputable dealers, and even national companies who cheat on their customers (*see page 3*). Shame on them! In the meantime, ten of thousands of destructive termites have been left undetected to party round the clock in hundreds of Florida homes....

Homes like yours. Without my unique 57-POINT TERMITE & PEST CONTROL INSPECTION SYSTEM, your home will just sit there exposed to the ravages of all those crawling, chewing, wood-munching critters. Before you know it, days will have tuned into weeks, then months....then years. If your current termite company hasn't done the job it said it would, you won't discover the damage until it's too late. (Last year, for example, the cost for repairing termite damage in the U.S. came in at over $1.7 billion!)

Now you know why **you can't shop termite treatment on just price alone.** It doesn't make sense, neither for your pocket book nor your peace of mind. Just one overlooked infestation can result in thousands of dollars more that the so-called "savings".

One the other hand, consider this. As a home owner, think what you could say to a future buyer if your home came with a built-in *transferable* Termite Guarantee. One that lasts, not just for one, or even five years—but for a *lifetime!* I call it my.....

Renewable, Three-Phase LIFETIME Guarantee
(A Guarantee Unheard Of In The Industry!)

ONE. If, within *one* year of your first treatment, we uncover a new colony of drywood termites, I will re-tent your home for FREE *and* (not "or") REFUND YOUR MONEY.

TWO. If, during the first *five* years of your active service contract, we uncover live drywood termites, we will re-tent for FREE.

THREE. If, during the five years and any year thereafter of your active service contract, we uncover **live** drywood termites, we will re-tent for FREE—EVEN IF YOU SELL THE HOME AND MOVE OUT!

Can you see how much added value that would bring to your home? Think of how you can impress a buyer with treatment and inspection records. Records going back several years. Or, if not years, then a service contract from a reliable termite company you can TRUST. A *transferable* service contract with a guarantee *unheard of in the industry.*

You want more proof? You're not sure of this "trust" idea? (Okay, I confess, I'm in a business that has earned little respect in the trust department.) Even so, you think I'm just saying all this just to get my next termite job? Well, scan your eyes over the following:

FIGURE 15.3: Chet Rowland's Sales Letter

FOR WRITTEN PEST-FREE HOME GUARANTEE, PLEASE SEE OTHER SIDE OF THIS PAGE.

How Can We Absolutely Guarantee You A Pest Free Home And Keep That Promise, When Most Other Pest Control Companies, Even "Big Names", Have All Kinds Of Sneaky Fine Print And Escape Clauses In Their Contracts, Pile Up Consumer Complaints At The Better Business Bureau, And Simply Fail To Honor Their Promises?

Yes, the guarantees on the other side of this page are real, straightforward and have been honored for 23 years, as we've served well over 37,000 Florida customers. Many stay with us for life. 92% of our new business comes from referrals. Why? Because, on top of very courteous and reliable service by the most experienced technicians in the industry, my company flat-out delivers on its guaranteed promise of a pest-free home. How can we do that? A big part of the answer is MY UNIQUE 17-STEP PEST CONTROL TREATMENT SYSTEM THAT SIMPLY LEAVES BUGS NO PLACE TO HIDE.

Look, a lot of companies spray some gunk around and that's about it. Watch any other company's people at work and see if they match up with MY treatment system:

INITIAL CLEAN-OUT
Step 1.   57-Point Pest & Termite Audit
Step 2.   Dust or bait attic and/or crawl spaces
Step 3.   Remove switch plates and electrical outlets, then apply appropriate dust/baits, etc.
Step 4.   Drill and treat kick plate holes under cabinets, vanities

INTERIOR TREATMENT
Step 5.   Inject cracks and crevices in kitchen, bathrooms
Step 6.   Treat around ALL doors and windows
Step 7.   Pull back plumbing covers in tub, showers, under sinks
Step 8.   Treat under and around all appliances
Step 9.   Treat around top and bottom of garage or carport
Step 10. Remove spider webs
Step 11. Look for any new termite mud tubes around garage expansion joints

EXTERIOR TREATMENT
Step 12. Treat ALL eaves and soffits
Step 13. Remove spider webs, even wasp nests
Step 14. Treat around ALL doors and windows
Step 15. Treat around garbage cans, wood piles, under decks
Step 16. Treat 6-foot "steel curtain defense barrier" around outside perimeter of your home
Step 17. Check for new termite mud tubes, wings of swarming termites

OUR $50.00 AND $100.00 CHALLENGES:
1.   Have us come and do this 17-Point Inspection with you watching, right after any other pest control company has provided their regular service. If we don't find and point out to you important bug-entry points or breeding ground left unprotected or untreated, we'll pay you $100.00.
2.   Watch closely as any other pest control company's technician provides your regular service—if he does all 17 of these things, and you will sign an affidavit to that effect, we'll pay you $50.00.

Even more detailed information about this 17-Point Inspection is available at www.chetspest.com or in a brochure available on request.

QUESTION: "CAN I GET BY WITH A LESS THOROUGH AND CHEAPER SERVICE?"
Maybe. But you'll find our prices are about in the middle of the market, not the cheapest but definitely not the highest, and there are NEVER hidden charges or surprises, or "low ball" quotes then lots of "up-selling." Our 23 years in business and over 37,000 customers say: our prices are fair. More importantly, the costs of settling for a "bottom-barrel", cheap service that basically just sprays one chemical around can be very, very high—from just the annoyance of paying every months and still having bugs to kill yourself, still pulling the can of store-bought bug spray our from under the sink…to having termites do very serious damage before you know what hit you. Saving a dollar or two and settling for less than our proven, superior service really is no bargain at all.

©2004 Proven Marketing Works

FIGURE 15.4: Chet Rowland's Sales Letter

OUR EXCLUSIVE IRON-CLAD, NO WIGGLE ROOM, SIMPLE, STRAIGHTFORWARD GUARANTEES.

Basically, I guarantee you will have a pest-free home and be 100% satisfied with every aspect of our services or I'll make it right or I'll refund 100% of your money. You will not find ANY company willing to match these guarantees. Here are the details:

GUARANTEE #1: Within 30 Days: Get Your UN-Deposited Payment Back
GUARANTEE #2: Within 60 Days: Get Your Money Back

If, after your first treatment, you are not fully satisfied anytime within 30 days, we will do a full re-treatment FREE OF CHARGE and make everything right, OR, if you prefer, I'll hand you back your UN-deposited check, cash or tear up you UN-processed credit card voucher. I take ALL the risk for the first month. I do NOT even deposit your payment for that first month. Only after you've seen for yourself that you really do have a pest-free home and you are completely satisfied, do I deposit your first payment.

Now, suppose that month passes but then you discover a few bugs are still there, in your home. That should NOT be the case. And as long as you call within TWO MONTHS, I'll send my top technicians out AGAIN-FREE- to again re-treat your entire home. And then if we still cannot satisfy you, I will still refund every penny you paid. If it takes THREE treatments to get your home pest-free, you'll get 'em. If you want your money back, you'll have it. You're the boss.

Frankly, there's no way on earth I could afford to do this—unless I was successful at making homes just like yours pest-free and at keeping customers for life. Which I am. So, take note: There's not fine print here. No little asterisk marks like this (*) with footnotes in tiny type. No "weasel clauses". No attorney language. I guarantee your satisfaction period. And, incidentally, I have a standing offer for any other pest control company: Prove that you've matched and honored an identical guarantee for at least 5 years in this area and I'll donate $500.00 to any charity of their choice.

Signed:

Chet Rowland

CHET ROWLAND
Owner
Chet's Pest Control

FIGURE 15.5: Chet Rowland's Sales Letter

NO ONE ELSE IN MY INDUSTRY MAKES THESE BOLD GUARANTEES!!!

	Chet's Termite & Pest Management	Other Pest Control Companies
1. Money Back Guarantee	ALWAYS	Never
2. Educate Customers	AL WAYS	Never
3. Lifetime Renewable Warranty	YES	No
4. Spot Treat	NO	Yes
5. Free Timbor Treatment of Attic and/or crawl space	YES	No
6. Free Furniture Fumigation	YES	No
7. Only Out Of Structure 48 to 52 Hours	YES	No
8. Leave Fumigant in Tent 20-24 Hours	ALWAYS	Seldom
9. Has Different Crew Introduce Fumigant	NEVER	Usually
10. Employees Held Accountable	ALWAYS	Never
11. Know Who Is Doing Your Service	AL WAYS	Never
12. Owner Is Accessible	AL WAYS	Never
13. Owner Has 30 Years Experience	YES	Never
14. Owner Personally Trains Crews	AL WAYS	Never
15. Supervisor Has 20 Years Experience	YES	Never
16. Measure Structure Accurately W /Wheels & Poles	ALWAYS	Seldom
17. Use Numerous Industrial Fans	ALWAYS	Never
18. Use Boat Tarps	NEVER	Always
19. Dig Up Your Yard	NEVER	Always
20. Holes In Tarps	NEVER	Always
21. Sew Seams All The Way Up And Down	YES	No
22. Seal Wires, Walls and TV Antennae, etc.	ALWAYS	Never
23. Use Sub-Contractor	NEVER	Sometimes
24. Follow Up Survey	YES	No
25. Referral Programs	AL WAYS	Never
26. Deliver Work As Promised	AL WAYS	Never

BENEFITS YOU DESERVE WHEN USING CHET'S TERMITE PEST MANAGEMENT

©2004 Proven Marketing Works

FIGURE 15.6: Chet Rowland's Refund Letter and Check

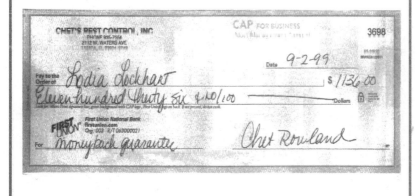

To Chet's Termite and Pest Control:

On February 12, 1999, Chet's Termite & Pest Control tented my house for drywood termites at 3112 W. Lambright in Tampa, Fl. 33614.

On May 13, 1999, we discovered new wings and asked for someone to come out and take a look. Live drywood termites were found at the time of your inspection and we scheduled to have our home re-tented on August 19, 1999.

On September 2, 1999, I received my money back for the tent fumigation of my home.

Needless to say I was thrilled that I didn't have to argue or threaten you to uphold your money back guarantee. Rest assured, I will tell my friends and others about how fair, honest and pleasant your company was to do business with. I will certainly use your services in the future when needed.

Lodia Lockhart

FIGURE 15.7: Chet Rowland's Refund Letter and Check

July21, 2000

Chet's Termite & Pest Control
2112 W Waters Avenue
Tampa, FL 33604

Attn: Chet Rowland

Dear Mr. Rowland,

On August 28, 1988, your service manager Duke Covington came out to our home at 1010 E. Mohawk in Tampa, Fl. 33604 to give us an Estimate to have our home fumigated for drywood termites. We Knew about your 100% money back guarantee if I were to get termites back within 1 year of the treatment date, and I felt confident contracting your company to take care of my termite problem.

On November 12, 1999, I had my home fumigated by your company. In June 2000 we discovered a suspicious area in the paneling of the front room and called your company back to investigate the problem. On June 9,2000, your service manager Duke Covington again came to our home to take a look at the problem. During the investigation Mr. Covington found that we did have live drywood termites in that area and instructed us to call your office to schedule and have the tenting done again and inquired about the money back guarantee.

On July 17, 2000 your company re-tented our home free of charge and on July 22, 2000 I picked up a check representing the amount we paid for the fumigation of our home.

We are very pleased to say that we received our money back within 1 week without having to threaten or harass your company to honor your claim of a money back guarantee. I will certainly tell friends and others about the honest, fair dealing we have had with your company and we hope to use your services again in the future if the need arises.

Shirley Rogers
Dan & Shirley Rogers

CHET'S PEST CONTROL, INC
PHONE 935-7554
2112 W. WATERS AVE
TAMPA, FL 33604-2748

CAP FOR BUSINESS
Asset Management Account

3188

Date 7-21-00

Pay to the Order of *Shirley Rogers* $ 803.00

Eight Hundred three and/100   Dollars

First Union National Bank
firstunion.com

For *Money back warranty (garantee)*   *Chet Rowland*

©2004 Proven Marketing Works

Systems for Every Marketer

There are many moving parts to good direct marketing, as you are no doubt realizing from reading this book, if you weren't already aware of it. To succeed, you ultimately have to fit the pieces together into systems. Then, the rubber meets the road with implementation. This next chapter presents a collection of technology tools that speed and support that implementation.

Regardless of the type of business, professional practice, or sales career you are involved in, these tools can make your life easier by making your marketing much more effective.

CHAPTER 16

How to Automate Your Marketing
Ron Romano

One of the objections many business owners have about using direct marketing is time. They say they don't have time to implement it. However, a great deal of this kind of marketing, from lead generation to follow-up, can be completely automated—essentially, done for you by "robots!"

Regardless of what your business is, what you sell, or how you sell it, making a sale is actually a multistep process. Customers or clients must first be interested prospects, and interested prospects are developed from leads. If you fully grasp this simple reality, you may very well change your ideas about what you do and don't have time for, and what your number-one job is.

So let me ask you: what is *your* number-one job in *your* business?

When I pose this question to many business groups, I get a variety of answers:

$$\$\$\$\$\$ \uparrow Sale \uparrow Customer \uparrow Prospects \uparrow Leads$$

- Some said to manage their business and their employees.
- Others believed dealing with suppliers—buying right and getting product on time—was critical to their success.
- Still others believed that they must keep their companies poised as industry leaders in technology or bringing on new and innovative products.
- Some replied staying on top of customer service so their customers would purchase again and again.
- A lot of people who were in small businesses answered, "Selling, it's my job to make the money."

All of these things are important to the success of any business. Anyone who has a business or is responsible for a business will be conscious of every aspect of it, but we all gravitate to certain things that are of special interest or are comfortable to us. And, while it's true that we are ultimately responsible for just about everything that happens in our businesses, there is one thing that must happen before *everything* else!

Before anything happens you need LEADS!

My partner, Michael, and I have this discussion all the time. Michael has been responsible for developing some of the most sophisticated hardware and software solutions that are integrated into our proprietary Turn-Key Automated Marketing Systems. There is no other company in North America that offers all of these systems. There is no other company that has automated all of these processes together. He is extremely proud of this, right-fully so, but . . . the technology is useless, unless we have a customer who uses it.

So, one again let's face reality . . .

You Need a System for Generating and Managing Leads

Nothing can happen in your business unless you are getting a steady stream of leads, have a good system that will sift, sort, and prequalify those leads so you only get qualified prospects, and have an excellent follow-up system that converts your prospects to customers . . . who become repeat customers because you stay in touch with them, building relationships of trust and confidence.

You can be the best cook, the best mechanic, the best chiro-practor, best dentist, best salesman, the best in any category. That does not always translate into your business being success-ful. I know lots of great chefs whose restaurants went bankrupt; there are lots of great chiropractors who are barely making ends meet.

So how do you attract a steady stream of leads, sift, sort, and prequalify, stay in touch with prospects automatically, and then build relationships that turn them into customers for life?

The secret that answers this question is in understanding the sale itself. When someone buys something, it is a PROCESS, not an EVENT.

A Sale Is a Process, Not an Event

Let me give you a quick example. It's hot—say about 95 degrees outside, sunny and muggy. You're walking down the street, and the heat's coming off the pavement like hot coals. Suddenly you walk past a Baskin-Robbins. You stop in your tracks; you start thinking, "I'm hot, a cold ice cream cone would taste mighty good right now." You look inside and see all the different flavors of ice cream. Then, you say to yourself, "I'm going to get one!" That was a process, albeit a short one. When you buy a plasma TV, furniture, house, car, etc., the process takes much longer.

Let's look at how that relates to our advertising. Most people advertise their products and services because they want the business NOW! That means they are appealing only to the person who is at the end of the buying process. That totally eliminates anyone who is at an earlier stage in the buying process.

Bad Idea!

If you advertise in a manner that only appeals to people at the end of the buying process, you waste the majority of your ad dollars. You may get some immediate buyers, but you leave behind lots of other prospects who could be developed into buyers through follow-up if first captured as leads. Look at it this way, if all you do is advertise for immediate buyers, you may be getting 5 cents of value for every $1.00 you spend on advertising.

Of course, if you alter your advertising to attract both immediate buyers and a lot of extra leads for follow-up, you will burden your business and its staff with a lot more people calling or coming in, and you could wind up with chaos, frustrated employees, and poor customer service. Somehow, you have to separate immediate buyers from leads and handle each differently.

If your marketing actually works, now you've created another problem for yourself. The phone's probably ringing like crazy. You don't have the manpower or the time to treat each call with the same friendly service to get those callers into your store to make the sale. Or worse yet, your staff is getting peeved at the calls because they're really busy and it's interrupting them, so they blow-off those potential customers.

Good Idea!

What if you had a way that offered those who were interested in your products or services a way to get information/the perfect pitch on how you will help them solve their problems in a non-threatening manner? (That means they don't have to talk to someone who is going to try to sell them something, so you get three to ten times the calls you would normally.) And then, the prospects gave you all their contact information so you could keep in touch with them automatically, giving them helpful information that solved all their problems and satisfied their needs, wants, and desires. Wouldn't that make your life easier?

Better Idea!

What if this automated robot delivered the perfect sales presentation every time and worked for you 24/7? And, as long as this automated robot is doing this, let's tell him to track all of the advertising so you know what works and what doesn't, which means you're not wasting thousands of dollars on ads that don't pull. Of yeah, we might as well tell this robot to stay in touch with these prospects regularly because they did raise their hands telling us they were interested, so they are somewhere in the buying cycle.

And when they convert to customers, let's clone ourselves with an automated robot that calls all our clients for us, in our voice, so we can stay in touch with them, building a personal relationship, which gets them to purchase from us with more regularity and frequency.

Work Less, Earn More

Does this sound like something every business should have? Imagine having Automated Marketing Systems working for you, getting more leads, tracking your ads, and staying in touch with all your prospects and clients.

Have you ever been told to work hard and you will be rewarded? That's exactly what my father told me when I started to work in the family business after graduating. Well, I worked hard for 14 years, putting in long hours, nights and weekends, never taking a vacation longer than a week every year, and when my dad passed away, what I was rewarded with was a bankrupt business.

I spent the next 15 years looking for the thing that was going to make me the money. I had a couple of different companies, but what I really had was a job because the company didn't function without me—and I lived month to month.

One company my partner and I started about a decade ago was a technology company that provided systems that marketers were using to get more leads and track marketing campaigns. Over that period, we have been fortunate enough to work with some of the top marketers in the world. We learned that they were all using a system, and that all of the processes and steps were basically the same.

The Secret Discovered . . .

But . . . there was one thing missing in their systematized approach to marketing, and that was the way technology was developed. The technology companies said, "Here's the technology, fit your marketing into it." What the marketers were looking for was the technology to fit their marketing.

All along I thought I was looking for the thing, and as it turns out, it was the system that makes money, not the thing. With the right system, any worthy product or service, anything can be profitably sold. Without the right system, many people selling a worthy thing will still struggle or fail.

Based on this discovery and this need shared by all savvy marketers, we went to work developing an approach to "marketing friendly technology" that led to our present large, growing business and the systems now used by hundreds of thousands of sales professionals and business owners. Here I'll tell you about the three most important systems used by virtually all of our clients. Those three automated moneymaking systems are:

1. Internet marketing systems
2. Stay-In-touch broadcasting systems
3. Toll-free recorded messages

These systems can be used and integrated into the marketing of any business. In fact, these systems are used in the same manner in over 100 business categories that our company services. Businesses like real estate (including commercial, residential, and investors), automotive, restaurant, chiropractic, insurance, financial, dentists, lawyers, cosmetic surgeons, pest control, carpet cleaners, garden centers, cemetery/funeral, bowling centers, men's and women's retail, and the list goes on. They are tested and proven to increase response, especially when used with the techniques in direct response marketing.

Internet Marketing Systems

Most business owners have a real love-hate relationship with the internet. They know they need a web site, it usually costs a ton of money, and no one can quantify their return on investment (ROI). To top it off, not many of us know how to keep the site updated or make quick changes. So it ends up either being an extended version of your business card or a time-sucking frustration where you spend a lot of time for very little monetary return.

Why do some people make a fortune on the internet and others virtually nothing? What's the big secret to cracking the internet vault to get at the riches inside?

It's pretty simple, if we just define what the internet is. The internet is just another marketing medium—that's it. It's just like newspapers, radio, TV, or direct mail. It's there for you to capture leads. Now here's the real bonus, when you integrate the medium—the internet—with technology, not only can you capture leads, you can also sequentially market to these leads automatically, either through e-mail or regular mail, until they die or buy! You can also send out a marketing campaign instantly at virtually no cost. And if you use your offline marketing effectively, you can double or triple the number of leads from any campaign.

The key is to set up real internet marketing systems as opposed to just a web site. If you follow the top internet marketers, you'll find they're all using the same system:

- Have multiple e-mail capture devices, usually linked to information that the visitor wants to solve his/her problems.

- Have devices tied to auto-responders.
- Incorporate sequential e-mail follow-up steps.
- Have a database storage facility within the web site so a marketing campaign can be created and sent.
- Incorporate audio on the site, which usually works well with testimonials.
- Have an easy-to-use wizard-like function that allows your mom to go in and make changes.
- Have multiple sites that offer single-page solutions so as not to distract the visitor with other information or have the visitor trying to find some particular information that is a benefit to them.
- Have multiple sites or addresses to track different marketing campaigns.

> ## Resource
>
> To view some samples of different kinds of internet marketing systems that work, go to www.IMSthatwork.com. These systems capture loads, consequently follow, and convert prospects to profits.

You should never make *all* your information available to the visitor. You spend your time, effort, and money to get them there, so you should be capturing their information to track, follow up, and convert to customers.

Stay-in-Touch Broadcasting Systems

Does it cost more money to get a new customer or market to an existing base of customers? Everyone knows the answer—it's less costly marketing to a base of customers. That's because we are talking to a narrower target group, those who have purchased from us before, who hopefully trust us, and who we know have a need for what we provide.

Here's the truth of the matter, all of us spend more time and money chasing new business than working on our base. I don't have the answer as to why that is, but I do have the answer on how to fix the problem with very little time and effort.

Call Them and They Will Come

One of the cheapest ways to get some instant sales is to call our customers. By cheap, I mean we didn't have to spend any cash. It's not so cheap if you factor in the time that's required to make all those phone calls. Not to mention, most of the time we're going to get an answering machine if we call during the day, and if you call at night, you're not going to be very popular.

My main point is that if we called our customers regularly, that would build a more personal relationship with each one of them, and we would sell more. Our customers now have a feeling of being "special," a feeling that we care about their business and it is important to us. This is the same thing we do to build any relationship—we communicate with that person on a regular basis. And all things being equal, people want to do business with family and friends. After all, aren't those the people we should be able to trust?

Here's our dilemma: It's a monumental task to call our customers, so at most we mail them and hope they open the mail. But it's not the same as a personal call.

Now picture making one phone call and delivering what appears to be your personal message, to all of your customers—simultaneously. Let me give you a couple of examples:

> Hi, this is Ron from Ron's Menswear. Sorry I missed you . . .
> just wanted to let you know about our semiannual suit sale that's
> happening this Friday and Saturday . . . and I just wanted to make
> sure you received our flier in the mail so our existing customers,
> like you, can take advantage of the sale prices before we
> advertise them in the paper. Hope to see you there. Bye.

This technology is cheap and effective. It usually boosts response by at least 30%.

> Hi, this is Ron from Ron's Automotive. Sorry I missed you . . .
> just wanted to wish you and your family a Happy Thanksgiving.
> We've got a lot to be thankful for, and we're especially thankful
> for all of our great customers, like you. If you need to call us,
> our number is (123) 456-7890.

A short message like the one above can start to build a relationship that sometimes will even guilt them into doing business with you.

There are many applications for this cheap and easy to use technology . . . and it's quick to implement. You can think of an idea tonight, send it tomorrow, and start to see results immediately.

Toll-Free Recorded Messages

A toll-free recorded message has a prerecorded message that prospects can call 24/7. You will get many more calls because you let your prospect know that:

- the number is toll-free (no charge to the caller),
- it is a prerecorded message (nonthreatening for the caller, they don't have to talk to any pushy salespeople),

- they can call anytime, 24 hours a day.

Here are a couple of examples of how to use toll-free recorded messages in your marketing:

Find Out the 87 Things You Need to Know—and Must Get
Done—When a Loved One Passes Away. For your Free Report,
call our 24-Hour, Prerecorded Toll-Free Hotline @ 1-800-xxx-xxxx,
ID #2001.

Find Out How to Eliminate Back Pain Forever.
Call Our Toll-Free 24-Hour Prerecorded Hotline to Get Your
Free Report @ 1-800-xxx-xxxx, ID #1234.

Find Out the 6 Common Homebuyer Mistakes That Could Cost
You Thousands of Dollars—and How to Avoid Them. Call Our
Toll-Free 24-Hour Prerecorded Hotline to Get Your Free Report
@ 1-800-xxx-xxxx, ID #1234.

By offering FREE INFORMATION that solves your prospects' needs, wants, and desires . . . and by giving them a nonthreatening (meaning they don't have to talk to a salesperson) way to get the solution to their problems, you will increase the number of people who will respond to your offer.

Not only do you increase response, but there are a number of benefits related to using these types of marketing systems.

Benefits of Toll-Free Recorded Messages That Will Double Your Profits!

1. Because prospects call your recorded message and leave their contact information, you get a list of all the prospects who are interested in your services. Now you can send

them information on a regular basis that keeps you at the top of their minds when they actually decide to make purchases, and you have positioned yourself as the knowledgeable expert in your field. What a BONUS! Imagine if you had the names, addresses, and phone numbers of everyone who called and said they were interested when you ran an ad.

2. Inherent in the technology are tracking devices so you get reports on the total number of people who called, the telephone number of the caller, which is captured automatically, how long they listened to your message, and if they left a message, which you can be notified of instantly. And, your information can be sent out by the automated robot without your ever having to do anything. By tracking calls on your ads, you know which ones work and which ones don't. This will not only save you a ton of money on inefficient ads but will make your marketing campaigns produce more sales because prospects are raising their hands and identifying themselves to you for follow up.

3. Recorded messages not only drive more calls, they can answer more calls with the perfect presentation every time. Let's face it, you advertise so that you'll get more calls. If you generated 30% more calls on your next ad, could you spend the time needed to handle those calls so the prospects would come into your business? How many times have you called a business about a product or service only to be put on hold forever, been treated abruptly by the person at the other end of the line, or told they would call you back, which never happened? Using recorded messages gives you the opportunity to record and give a

perfect presentation to every caller, no matter if it's 1 call or 50 simultaneously.

4. You have a huge advantage over your competition. Just think if you went to the Yellow Pages right now and were trying to decide on which company to call about a certain product or service. Which business do you call based on their ad? For everyone who calls the big ad, someone prefers the small ad. Someone likes the blue one, and another the red one. People even make decisions based on the business name. Toll-free recorded messages give prospects a REASON WHY they should call. If you were looking for a mechanic to fix your car by surfing the Yellow Pages—and one ad had a heading, "Before You Hire an Auto Mechanic, Find Out the 6 Questions You Must Ask to Make Sure You Don't Get Ripped Off . . . Call Our 24-Hour Recorded Message Hotline @ 1-800-123-4567," do you think you would call? Of course you would. Now you get a chance to give a perfect sales pitch outlining reasons why they should come to you.

Three Leverage Points

You can only make so much money through work. So, you try to get leverage. For most businesses, there are three chief leverage opportunities:

1. People
2. Marketing/media
3. Technology

Most business owners do a good job with PEOPLE. They have employees, they may have salespeople, they may have people working in multiple outlets, and they may sell their products through others' stores, staffed by people.

With the information in this book, Dan Kennedy's other books, and all the web sites and other resources in this book, you can do a better job leveraging marketing and media.

But most business owners fall short when it comes to leveraging technology. It's important to invest more time in getting this right, even if it's uncomfortable for you, because your ability to get maximum leverage and benefit out of people and marketing/media is directly affected by your use of technology. And now you know you can actually *automate* your marketing with the right technology for even greater leverage!

Ron Romano is president of Automated Marketing Solutions, the leading provider of integrated, automated marketing systems and technology. For more information, visit www.findmeleads.com, fax (800) 294-5321, or call (800) 858-8889.

Customer Retention

When most people think of marketing, they think in terms of attracting and acquiring *new* leads, prospects, customers, clients or patients. This next chapter addresses something every bit as important: keeping the customers you have.

CHAPTER 17

How to Put a Fence
Around Your Customers
Dan Kennedy

I f you have a big herd of cows, you might be an easy prospect for a new, whizbang sort of milking machine to that might get an extra drop of milk from each teat. You could easily do the math:

x# cows x 1 extra drip

= y# more gallons of milk per day

x $Z per gallon x 365 days in a year

= Total Added Income – cost of machine

= Net Profit.

Phone: (602) 997-7707
Office Phone Answered "Live By Staff"
Only Wednesday Afternoons AZ Time
FAX: (602) 269-3113

DAN S. KENNEDY
Rancher

5818 N. 7th Street #103
Phoenix, Arizona 85014
www.dankennedy.com

You might be an easy prospect to sell all kinds of advertising to: promote your brand of milk, get more stores to stock your milk, and get more people to drink your milk.

You might buy better trucks and other equipment. You might buy better nutritional products for the cows. You'll pay whatever the veterinarian asks of you.

But if your fence is in disrepair, and all your cows get loose and wander off or stampede, what good is all that other stuff?

I try to teach business owners to think of themselves as I do, as ranchers putting together and taking care of herds of good, responsive customers. That's the only real asset of a business.

For that farmer, it's not so easy to do the math for the fence.

Most marketers do a truly terrible job of keeping a fence around their customers in tip-top shape. Just like the farmer, they view it as an "expense of operations," whereas I view it as "marketing."

I believe you should spend at least as much, if not more, per year on the fence as you did on acquiring the customer in the first place.

Further, you should remember there are poachers and rustlers trying to steal your customers every single day. If you leave your customers alone for very long, if they feel ignored or underappreciated, they are more easily lured away.

What Is a "Fence"?

In marketing terms, a fence can be "manufactured" of several things. Under utopian conditions, there is some pain, fear or loss of disconnect. Switching from cable TV to satellite TV, for example, carries with it not just expense but worry about inconvenience, the new thing not working, missing your favorite channels. The telephone and utility companies have even stronger pain of disconnect. But there can be pain of disconnect engineered into all sorts of businesses where it's not so obvious. It can even be purely about the relationship. The fence can also be manufactured from product quality, service excellence, convenience of location, brand preference, and many other things. But I want to talk here about the *maintenance* of the fence. How do you maintain such a good fence that rustlers can't get in, that customers never leave?

The 52X Contact Program

Fence maintenance is about repetition, frequency, and quality of communication.

I prescribe 25 to 52 "touches" per year, NOT including outright offers, sales pitches, or transactions. With the advent of virtually free e-mail, many astute marketers have added that on to take 52 to several hundred! For example, if you are a Glazer-Kennedy Inner Circle Member, you are getting the newsletter you subscribe to every month and the audio CD every month. You may be getting a free e-mail marketing tip everyday. You may be getting a weekly fax. You'll get a seasonal greeting. You may get several gift books during the year, in total, 24 to as many as 250 touches during the year!

Most businesses' touches may include a Christmas and/or Thanksgiving greeting or gift, a birthday greeting or gift, a card commemorating the anniversary of your first doing business together, and an annual customer appreciation event promotion. It's easy to find and plan for about a dozen of these kinds of touches during the year. Many of the top marketers who've contributed to this book multiply each of these occasions with more than one media. For example, Scott Tucker sends his mortgage customers a Happy St. Patrick's Day card in the mail but also delivers a phone message via automation (as described in Ron Romano's chapter).

In addition to these sorts of things, my single biggest recommendation is the use of a monthly customer newsletter (or, for the really ambitious, more than one).

Nothing, and I mean nothing, maintains your fence better. Because it arrives every month, it is looked at as a "publication," not just a promotion. And if it's content is correct, customers look forward to receiving it. You get frequency. You have a good self-imposed discipline of a monthly publication. And this is an opportunity to do something else that's very important: deliver entertaining, interesting information, not just offers and sales pitches.

If you prepare your own from scratch, you can use it as an opportunity to continually strengthen your positioning as an expert, as a trusted advisor, as well as a fun and interesting person. But no one's customer newsletter should be all about his business. If you're a property and casualty insurance agent, you need to realize no one's quite as interested in insurance as you are! Actually, the customer newsletters that work best have a lot of *"Readers Digest* lite" kind of content, like trivia, quizzes, games, recipes, celebrity news, and very general tips about health, home, money, or business.

Because most businesspeople simply cannot be motivated and goaded into doing their own customer newsletters from scratch every month, I developed a "prefab" newsletter that just about anybody can use. There are two versions: *Good News*, to be sent to consumers, and *Good Business News*, to be sent to business owners. For a very small fee, the business owner gets this on a disc every month, drops in his identity and an offer of the month, and has the local printer put it out for them. Or my publisher will even take care of everything: the customization, printing, and mailing.

> ### Resource
>
> To get information about using Dan's Good Newsletters for your business, contact DONE4YOU PUBLISHING, c/o PeteThePrinter.com or call or fax (330) 922-9833.

With these newsletters, I've combined the "lite content" I just described with a very deliberate and strategic effort to make people feel better about themselves and more confident about the economy. You can see from the samples at the end of this chapter (Figures 17.1 and 17.2) how I've done this. The newsletters also contain exclusive, branded Dan Kennedy content, so the business owner is linked to me and is bringing his customers or clients my information and ideas.

Don't Be Dumb, Lazy, or Cheap About This!

In the 25 years I've been pushing and prodding and cajoling and nagging business owners to put out a newsletter (or newsletters!)

to their customers, believe me, I've heard every excuse and objection!

"Why every month? That's a lot.
How about four times a year?"

No. Every month. Your magazines arrive every month. Real publications are monthly. Plus, in three months, your fence can rot, weaken, and fall apart. Rustlers lurking outside waiting for the first chance they can get'll be inside your fence. You want to arrive in your customers' mailboxes every month to say hi, bring some good cheer, deliver some useful tips and information, remind them you're ready to serve them, thank people for referrals, and make a special offer. Every month. After all, which month don't you want your customers coming back or referring others?

"It's too expensive."

If you can't or won't invest about $25.00 to $30.00 a year per customer in keeping your fence in tip-top shape, I suggest getting out of the ranching business altogether. Bluntly, frankly, either you're a financial nitwit or you've managed to round up a spectacularly worthless herd. Even if you could not directly trace a dollar in sales to this, you must do it to maintain the fence. But while you may not measure your losses of customers wandering off or being rustled, you can measure the return on this investment, and almost everybody who does ranks it as their *best* marketing investment. Scott Tucker, for example, tells me that every single time he does a "touch," he stirs up refinancing business and referrals. Rory Fatt has hundreds of restaurant owners all reporting exact, tracked sales results from their newsletters. NOT doing this is much costlier than doing it.

"Why don't I just use e-mail. That's free."

I have a friend who gets her birthday greeting and Mother's Day greeting from one of her grown children via e-mail. She is always terribly disappointed. I don't blame her. Yes, e-mail has earned its place in the marketing tool kit. But it is no substitute for the arrival of a printed newsletter. Your customers get to "unwrap the present," they know you went to trouble and expense; they look forward to getting it; they actually read it (no delete button); they share it with family and friends.

"I can't write." "I'm too busy." "I don't have time."

The best answers are: learn, make time. It's important. In fact, nothing is more important than the fence, and the fence is essentially relationship. However, as I described earlier, I've solved this problem for you, with DONE4YOU newsletters you get to use as your own. One way or another, you NEED to get this done.

If you change nothing about your business as a result of this book, you would still have been well served if it succeeds at getting you to send a good monthly newsletter to your customers!

FIGURE 17.1: Good News Newsletter for Consumers

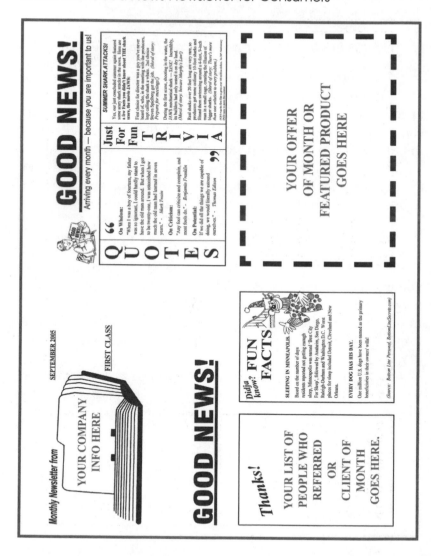

FIGURE 17.1: Good News Newsletter for Consumers

FIGURE 17.2: Good Business News Newsletter for Business Owners

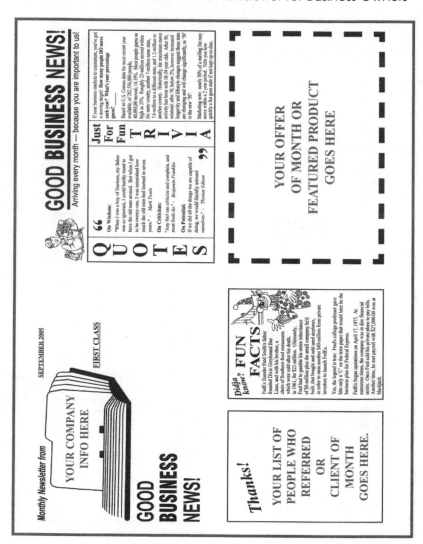

FIGURE 17.2: Good Business News Newsletter for Business Owners

RESOURCES

Resource Directory

I n this Resource Directory, you will find people mentioned in the book whom you might want to contact. (They are listed by page numbers.) A much more extensive, frequently updated Resource Directory is provided to all Glazer-Kennedy Inner Circle Members who receive my *No B.S. Marketing Letter*, and you can arrange a free three-month membership with no obligation at www.dankennedy.com.

People Included in this Book

Bill Glazer   Page 45
Phone: (800) 228-8178 (for Free Report)

Fax: 410-825-3301
Web site: www.bgsmarketing.com

Chauncey Hutter, Jr.   Page 55
Real Tax Business Success
Fax: (434) 984-1590
Web sites: www.chaunceyhutterjr.com and
www.thePROTAXfranchise.com

Rory Fatt   Page 79
Restaurant Marketing Systems
Fax: (604) 940-6902
Web site: www.myrestaurantcoach.com

Dr. Ben Altadonna   Page 91
Web site: www.benaltadonna.com.

Charles W. Martin DDS, MAGD, DICOI, FIADFE   Page 103
Phone: (866) 263-5577
Fax: (804) 320-1014
Web site: www.AffluentPracticeSystems.com

Al Williams   Page 117
Pacific Northwest Capital
Phone: (800) 265-3860
Fax: (206) 264-1327
Web site: www.apartmentfinancing.com

Scott Tucker   Page 127
Tucker Marketing Systems Inc.
Fax: (773) 327-2842
Web site: www.mortgagemarketinggenius.com

Chet Rowland   Page 139
Chet's Pest Control
Fax: (813) 926-06571
Web site: www. pcomillionaire.com.

Ron Romano   Page 153
Automated Marketing Solutions
Phone: (800) 858-8889
Fax: (800) 294-5321
Web site: www.findmeleads.com

Pete Lillo   Page 175
DONE4YOUPUBLISHING
Fax: (330) 922-9833
Web site: www.petetheprinter.com

Web Sites of Special Interest

www.nobsbooks.com

Information about all books in the No B.S. series, free sample chapters, bonus gifts for each book, and free e-mail courses for the *No B.S. Wealth Attraction* and *No B.S. Direct Marketing for NON-Direct Marketing Businesses* books.

www.dankennedy.com

Information about Dan Kennedy professional services, newsletters, and audio products. Also, Glazer-Kennedy Inner Circle annual Marketing and Moneymaking SuperConference and annual Information Marketers' Summit.

www.renegademillionaire.com

Information about Dan's Renegade Millionaire System and annual Renegade Millionaire Retreat.

www.nationalsaleslettercontest.com

Information about the sales letter/marketing plan contest, featuring a new Ford Mustang as top prize. No purchase required to enter.

www.petetheprinter.com

Home of DONE4YOU publications and services, including ready-to-use customer newsletters for any business, featuring Dan Kennedy content. Also, two special Dan Kennedy publications: *No B.S. INFO-Marketing Letter* (only for information marketers) and *Look Over Dan's Shoulder* (for direct response marketers and copywriters).

www.psycho-cybernetics.com

Dr. Maltz and Maltz/Kennedy publications.

www.entrepreneurpress.com
Official site of Entrepreneur Press.

www.northfieldpark.com

Dan's "home track," where he races his harness horses.

Need to Find
One of America's Leading Marketing
Experts for Your Type of Business?

Interested in a New or Additional
Business Opportunity?

Dan Kennedy's recommended experts, authorities,
business coaches, and consultants are featured
at www.renegademillionairemarketing.com

And in *Renegade Millionaire Magazine*, published twice
annually, online at this site.

Other Books by Dan Kennedy

The No B.S. Series

No B.S. Wealth Attraction for Entrepreneurs (Entrepreneur Press)

No B.S. Sales Success (Entrepreneur Press)

No B.S. Business Success (Entrepreneur Press)

No B.S. Time Management for Entrepreneurs (Entrepreneur Press)

Make Millions with Your Ideas (Plume)

The Ultimate Marketing Plan (Adams Media)

The Ultimate Sales Letter (Adams Media)

The New Psycho-Cybernetics with Dr. Maxwell Maltz (Pearson)

Zero Resistance Selling (Prentice-Hall/Pearson)

The Ultimate Success Secret (www.dankennedyproducts.com)

Why Do I Always Have to Sit Next to the Farting Cat? (petethe printer.com)

Complete Catalog of Audio Programs (www.nobsbooks.com)

About the Author

Dan S. Kennedy started in the advertising business in the early 1970s at a very young age, with no academic credentials, formal training, or apprenticeship. He has gone on to advise *Fortune* 500 and major brand-name corporations as well as thousands of entrepreneurs and small business owners; he has crafted and written ads, direct-mail campaigns, TV infomercials, and has created online marketing that has sold billions of dollars of goods and services. He has worked hands-on with clients in 156 different business categories, and helped hundreds of private clients become millionaires and multimillionaires, fast. His famous-name corporate clients have included

Weight Watchers International, Amway Corporation, Mass Mutual Insurance, Sun Securities, and Guthy-Renker Corporation, with infomercials and products including Pro-Activ, Victoria Principal Skin Care, and, in the information realm, *Personal Power*/Tony Robbins and *Think and Grow Rich*. Dan's network of industry-specialized consultants and business coaches directly works with over 500,000 business owners every year.

For more than 20 years, Dan was one of the most in-demand, popular, professional speakers in America on marketing topics, including nine consecutive years on the Success tour, addressing audiences of 10,000 to 35,000, repeatedly sharing the platform with former U.S. presidents, General Colin Powell, Hollywood celebrities, athletes, legendary entrepreneurs including Debbi Fields (Mrs. Fields Cookies) and Jim McCann (1-800-Flowers), and other top speakers Brian Tracy, Tom Hopkins, and Zig Ziglar.

His many business books have been featured in *Success Magazine, Entrepreneur* magazine, on *Inc.* magazine's 100 Best Business Books list, and on *Business Week* magazine's bestseller lists. (Information on all books is at www.nobsbooks.com.) The main newsletter he writes and edits, *The No B.S. Marketing Letter*, is the number-one paid subscription newsletter on direct marketing for all business owners in the world. (Information is at www.dankennedy.com.)

You can contact the author directly via fax at (602) 269-3113.

About the Other Authors

The authors in Section II are all Dan Kennedy students, clients, fabulously successful practitioners of Kennedy-style marketing, and in most cases, consultants, coaches, and advisors to different industries or professions. Brief biographies and contact information appear at the end of each chapter. Most of those authors have also contributed at greater length to the free e-mail course linked to this book (available at www.nobsbooks.com).

Index

Free Offers and Resources
from Dan Kennedy

Contest

**ENTER THE NATIONAL
SALES LETTER & MARKETING PLAN CONTEST**

Compete for a new FORD MUSTANG and other
exciting prizes!

Have your best sales letter/marketing plan evaluated
by a panel of expert judges.

No purchase required.

Contest is connected to two new 2006 books
by Dan Kennedy:
The Ultimate Sales Letter
and
The Ultimate Marketing Plan.

All rules, details, and free registration at:
www.NationalSalesLetterContest.com

Special Free Gift from the Author

THE MOST INCREDIBLE
FREE GIFT EVER

FAX: (410) 825-3301, ATTN: Darlene or
take advantage of this offer at www.freegiftfrom.com/dankennedy/

_____ **YES!** I want to take you up on The Most Incredible FREE Gift Ever" offer

Here's what you'll get:

* Six CD set of a Dan Kennedy Seminar entitled "Having the Confidence and Power to Achieve Maximum Dollars and Wealth. VALUE: $199.00
* Three Full Months of Dan Kennedy's "ELITE" Gold Membership. VALUE: $119.91
* Special Interview with Corey Rudl Entitled: How to Effectively Use the Internet to Market Your Business. VALUE: $239.99
* Special Interview With Robert Ringer, Author of "Action! Nothing Happens Until Something Moves." VALUE: $239.99
* Dan Kennedy's three times a week "Success Marketing Strategies: On-Line course. VALUE: PRICELESS

To take advantage of THE MOST INCREDIBLE FREE GIFT EVER you only pay a one-time charge of $19.95 (or $39.95 for Int'l subscribers) to cover postage (but this is for everything). Frankly, you've got to experience everything for yourself because anything I or anyone says just doesn't matter until you try it.

Then, after the FREE 3 months of receiving your 'ELITE' Gold Membership benefits, I will automatically charge you the lowest price that I offer Gold Membership, only $39.97 a month or $49.97 for Int'l subscribers. And here's the best part. If after the FREE 3 months, or anytime thereafter, you want to cancel your Membership, simply give us a call at 410-951-0147 or fax us a note at 410-825-3301 and my office will STOP charging your credit card immediately. No questions, no hassles, no hard feelings. You must be completely satisfied. If not, I want you to cancel your Membership.

NAME _____

BUSINESS NAME _____

ADDRESS (No P.O. Boxes) _____

CITY_____**STATE** _____ **ZIP**_____

PHONE _____**FAX** _____

EMAIL _____

CREDIT CARD ☐ Visa ☐ MasterCard ☐ American Express ☐ Discover

CREDIT CARD # _____·_____ **EXP. DATE** ___ / ___ / ___

SIGNATURE_____ **DATE** _____